Getting Started In

Jewish Genealogy

Gary Mokotoff & Warren Blatt

AVOTAYNU, INC., Bergenfield, NJ • 2000

Avotaynu, Inc.
P.O. Box 99
Bergenfield, NJ 07621

Printed in the United States of America

Library of Congress Cataloging-in-Publication Data

Mokotoff, Gary
Getting started in Jewish genealogy / by Gary Mokotoff and Warren Blatt.
p. cm.
Includes bibliographical references.
ISBN 1-886223-10-6
1. Jews—Genealogy—Handbooks, manuals, etc. I. Blatt, Warren. II. Title

CS21.M65 1999
929'.1'089924—dc21 99-052151

Contents

Introduction

Two major events shaped Jewish life of the past two hundred years: migration and the Holocaust. Few Jews today live where their ancestors lived a century or two ago. As a result, many Jews believe they cannot trace their family roots because:

Myths of Jewish Genealogy

• *Nobody remembers* anything about the family; no one is alive who can tell me about my family's past.

• *All the records were destroyed* in the Holocaust; my town was wiped off the map.

• *My family name was changed* (at Ellis Island); therefore, even if the records exist in my ancestral country, I do not know what names to search.

Facts about Jewish Genealogy

The statements above are myths. Jewish genealogy today is highly organized, and help is available to dispel these myths. There are many resources available to help you trace your Jewish family heritage.

• *Internet*. There is a strong presence of Jewish genealogy on the Internet; databases exist on the Internet to get you started.

• *Societies*. There are more than 80 Jewish genealogical societies throughout the world where you can meet other persons who are tracing their roots.

• *Books*. There are no less than 50 books useful to Jewish genealogy that can hone your skills and provide information that will lead you to records of your ancestors.

• *Magazine*. There is a quarterly magazine for Jewish genealogy: *Avotaynu: The International Review of Jewish Genealogy*.

• *Records*. While most things Jewish were destroyed in the Holocaust, vital and census records are government records. Despite the ravages of war in Europe during the past 200 years, most of these records have survived; you just have to know how to access them.

The purpose of this book is to get you jump-started in your genealogical research. It will lead you to other books, magazines, databases, and resources that will turn this ever-growing hobby into a pleasurable, rewarding experience.

This book had its genesis in *FAQ: Frequently Asked Questions About Jewish Genealogy* published on the Internet at <http://www.jewishgen.org/infofiles/faq.html> and published in book form by Avotaynu, Inc. in

1996. *FAQ* was authored by Warren Blatt. Gary Mokotoff expanded and reorganized that work to create *Getting Started in Jewish Genealogy*. It is not a beginners guide to Jewish genealogy; a number of larger works of that type are described in Appendix A. It is meant as an overview of how to do Jewish genealogical research. Furthermore, it is oriented toward the needs of Jews of Central or Eastern European ancestry who are living in the United States. Many portions apply to any Jewish genealogical research.

We would like to thank Barbara Lightbody, Eileen Polakoff, and Donna Tartasky for peer reviewing this book. Ruth Mokotoff edited and proofread the work.

Good luck in your research!

Warren Blatt
Gary Mokotoff

Getting Started: Interviewing People

Preparation

Start your family history research by interviewing people—starting with yourself—who have knowledge of the family's past. Before you interview people, decide what information you want to capture. Documenting each member of your family usually starts by writing down the vital information about each individual.

- Name: Given name, middle name, surname.
- Date and place of birth
- Date and place of marriage
- Date and place of death
- Date and place of burial

There is the question of which name to use. Here are some good rules. In the case of married women, the surname is the so-called maiden name at time of marriage. For example, if Edna Cohen married Samuel Finkelstein, she is shown on the tree as Edna Cohen, not Edna Finkelstein or Edna Cohen Finkelstein. If a person changed names during his/her lifetime, show the name as used today for living persons and the name at time of death for deceased persons. Document all other names for the individual; when you search for records, they may be found under these other names. For example, in searching for the birth record of an immigrant ancestor who changed his name from Yossel Tartasky to George Tarr, you would have to look for the birth of Yossel, not George.

For place names, there is a standard that too few people use. In the case of towns within the United States, specify town name/county/state. In the case of other countries, specify the town name/province/country. This is done because there leaves no doubt as to which town is being referenced. If you state a person was born in Brooklyn, we all know it is almost certainly Brooklyn, New York, but it could be Brooklyn, Maryland, so documenting the birth place as Brooklyn, New York, is more precise. If you elect to use the standard, properly it should read Brooklyn, Kings, New York, showing the city/county/state.

As is too often true of any documentation project, you will find in the middle of the project that there was data you wish you had collected from the first day, so it is recommended you also capture the following information.

- Birth name, if different from current name. Also other names during the person's lifetime
- Place of residence for living persons
- Religious name
- Namesake; who the person is named after

These last two points, religious name and namesake, will become increasingly important as you go back in time and start to encounter difficulties in identifying distant ancestors. Ashkenazic Jews, the Jews of Central and Eastern Europe, typically name their children after deceased relatives. By capturing the religious name for individuals, you will detect patterns that give clues to the names of more ancient ancestors. For example, if three brothers have children, and in each family there is a male child whose religious name is Eliyahu, all born within the same 10-year period, it is almost certain there was an ancestor named Eliyahu, not so distant from these male children—perhaps their grandfather.

Interviewing People

Where do you start? Start by interviewing every person who might have knowledge of your family's history. The first person to interview is yourself.

Document everything you know about your family according to the guidelines listed above; names, dates, and places. When you think you have gone as far as you can go, interview yourself as you would properly interview another person. Ask yourself:

- Do you have any documents or family memorabilia that might identify people or date such events as births, marriages, or deaths? Bar mitzvah certificates, wedding announcements, naturalization papers, and the like might contain information about your ancestors that you have forgotten.
- Do you have any old family pictures that would identify people or allow you to date such events as births, marriages, and deaths? A person interviewed by a genealogist stated he did not know the marriage date of his grandparents. Not more than 15 minutes later, he proudly displayed his grandparents' 50th wedding anniversary album that was dated 1941.
- Who you are named after? Ashkenazic Jews name their children after deceased ancestors. Who are your siblings named after? Your children?
- Whether events occurred during your lifetime. Approximate dates can often be deduced from events in your own life. You do not know when your great-grandfather died? Was he alive when you were born? If

so, did he attend your bat/bar mitzvah? Did he attend your wedding? Use this same technique when interviewing others.

Once you have exhausted all sources of information in your memory or possession, look at your family tree and ask which other members of the family might have information unknown to you. Don't forget to consider interviewing those who married into the family; they often remember information forgotten by family members. Interview them and ask the very same questions described above that you asked yourself. When interviewing them, use a tape recorder. Take notes and then compare your notes against the taped interview. You will be amazed how much information you forgot to write down. Listening to the interview again will also create a host of additional questions to ask. Never ask a person, "What do you know about the family's history?" Too often the response will be, "Nothing." Ask the questions listed above. Ask to see old photographs in the possession of the person you are interviewing. Ask to see old documents. Ask who the person being interviewed is named after. Ask about dates and places.

There are numerous books that can help you in your genealogical research. The book illustrated above provides hints for interviewing people.

Jump-Starting Using the Internet

The Internet is rapidly becoming a major conduit of information for Jewish genealogy. If you do not have access to it, find a friend or relative who can assist you. Alternately, most libraries have Internet access for their patrons. The Internet is that important a resource.

There are a number of databases available on the Internet that will jump-start your research by putting you in contact with individuals who have similar research interests, or making you aware of books or other databases that might contain information of use to you. Before you use these databases, it is important that you understand a concept called soundexing.

Soundexing: An Introduction

Lists of town names or surnames are usually provided in alphabetical order. However, it is not unusual for surnames or towns to have many spelling variations, usually phonetic variations, that cause these alternatives not to appear consecutively when presented in alphabetical order. The Consolidated Jewish Surname Index notes more than 140 spelling variants of the name Lipshitz[1] including Lapszyc, Lefshits, Libschuetz, Luboshitz, Lypszyc. Consider the consequence of trying to search a list of names for all spelling variants of Lipshitz.

Soundexing attempts to solve this problem by sequencing information by sound rather than by spelling. A soundex system combines letters of the alphabet that sound the same into a common code, usually a number. The soundex system used in all Jewish genealogical databases is called the Daitch-Mokotoff Soundex System. American records, such as census and passenger arrival records, use the American Soundex System. A complete description of both systems can be found on the Internet at <http://www.avotaynu.com/soundex.html>.

Briefly, the rules for the Daitch-Mokotoff Soundex System are the

[1] Lapshits, Lapszyc, Lebshutz, Lefschetz, Lefshetz, Lefshits, Leiboshetz, Leiboshits, Leibositz, Leibshitz, Leifschitz, Leipschitz, Leipsic, Lejboshits, Lejbshits, Lejbushets, Lejbuszyc, Lepschitz, Lepshetz, Levshets, Levshits, Lewszyc, Liboshits, Liboshutz, Libouschitz, Libschuetz, Libshets, Libshits, Libshitz, Libsitz, Libszyc, Libtsis, Libushits, Liebeschuetz, Lieboshitz, Liebschitz, Liebschuetz, Liebschutz, Liebschuz, Liebshutz, Liepschuetz, Lievshitz, Lifchis, Lifchits, Lifchitz, Lifchus, Lifchutz, Liffchitz, Liffshutz, Lifscheitz, Lifschitz, Lifschuetz, Lifschutz, Lifshets, Lifshits, Lifshitz, Lifshutz, Lifsitz, Lifszec, Lifszes, Lifszyc, Lipchic, Lipchitz, Lipchutz, Lipcicz, Lipczyc, Liphchitz, Liphshetz, Liphshitz, Lippschits, Lippschitz, Lippschuetz, Lippschutz, Lipschetz, Lipschitz, Lipschiz, Lipschuetz, Lipschutz, Lipscutz, Lipsetz, Lipshatz, Lipshchits, Lipshes, Lipshets, Lipshetz, Lipshez, Lipshits, Lipshits, Lipshitz, Lipshiz, Lipshotz, Lipshutz, Lipsich, Lipsics, Lipsits, Lipsitz, Lipsius, Lipsschitz, Lipsutz, Lipszec, Lipszes, Lipszic, Lipszyc, Liptsis, Lipzsycz, Lipzszyc, Lipzyc, Livchitz, Livschitz, Livschiz, Livshets, Livshich, Livshis, Livshits, Livshitz, Livshiz, Livsitz, Liwchez, Liwchitz, Liwschitz, Liwshitz, Liwszyc, Lobchitz, Lobositz, Lobschitz, Lobshits, Luboshez, Luboshitz, Luboszczyc, Luboszyc, Lubschutz, Lubshits, Luebschuetz, Luepschuetz, Luepshuetz, Lufschutz, Lupchutz, Lupshits, Luvashis, Luvishis, Luvshis, Lypszic

following. Take the word to be soundexed and drop all occurrences of vowels unless it is the first letter of the word. In the case of Lipshitz, you would be left with LPSHTZ. Take the remaining letters (consonants) and assign them numbers according to the following scheme (Note: This is an incomplete definition of the Daitch-Mokotoff Soundex system and is used for illustration only):.

0	A, E, I, O, U, J and Y at the beginning of a word
1	J, Y
2	ST
3	D, T
4	C, CZ, SH, SZ, S, TZ, Z
5	G, H, K, Q
6	M, N
7	B, F, P, V, W
8	L
9	R

Code only the first six remaining letters. If there are fewer than six letters coded, fill in the balance of the code with zeroes. Using the table above, the name Lipshitz (L-i-p-sh-i-tz) codes to 874400. What is more significant is that most other spelling variants of Lipshitz also code to 874400. Therefore, listing all names in the order of the six-digit Daitch-Mokotoff Soundex System rather than alphabetically will place all the spelling variants together.

When searching for a name, always use a soundex index, if available, rather than an alphabetical index. When dealing with computerized Jewish genealogical databases, you won't have to code the name yourself; the computer will do it for you.

Important Note

The first time you use any of the databases noted below, read the instructions at the Internet site that accompanies the database. It will save you time and minimize the risk that you might not locate information valuable to your research.

JewishGen Family Finder

The most valuable database to get you started is the JewishGen Family Finder (JGFF) [see example on page 62]. This is a list of surnames and towns being researched by more than 30,000 Jewish genealogists throughout the world. Its address is <http://www.jewishgen.

org/jgff>. Go to the JGFF site and see if other genealogists are researching your family name. In most cases, it will give you the person's e-mail address so you can contact the individual and jump-start your research. If you know the town from which your family came, also use JGFF to see if others are researching your town. Since a surname can be spelled different ways in different countries, change the SEARCH TYPE when using JGFF from "Standard" to the "Daitch-Mokotoff Soundex."

When writing to other researchers, give them a brief description of your family history. Example: "I am researching the Finkelstein family from Lublin, Poland, and noticed in the JewishGen Family Finder that you are researching that family name too. My Finkelsteins are the descendants of Abraham and Mollie Finkelstein who came to the United States about 1910. Their children were Abe, Hyman (Chaim), Peggy (Rivka), and Florence (Fayge), born in 1904, 1906, 1911, and 1914 respectively. Are we related? Is there any advice you can give me to help me in my research?"

If you are corresponding with a researcher because the person is researching the same town, your letter might say: "I am researching the Finkelstein family from Lublin, Poland, and noticed in the JewishGen Family Finder that you are researching the town of Lublin, also. My Finkelsteins are the descendants of Abraham and Mollie Finkelstein who came to the United States about 1910. Their children were Abe, Hyman (Chaim), Peggy (Rivka), and Florence (Fayge), born in 1904, 1906, 1911, and 1914 respectively. Where can I find additional information about the Jews of Lublin? I have already found information about the town in the *Encyclopedia Judaica*, on the Internet, and from interviews with family members."

In these examples, you have already demonstrated a conscientious attempt to do the research yourself. A standard joke in Jewish genealogy is the letter that says, "My family name is Cohen from Warsaw. What can you tell me about my family?" Such a letter will likely not be answered.

Consolidated Jewish Surname Index

The next step is to locate reference material that contains information about your family name. Go to the Consolidated Jewish Surname Index (CJSI) at <http://www.avotaynu.com/csi/csi-home.htm> [see example on page 63]. This is a database of more than 230,000 surnames, mostly Jewish, gleaned from 28 different sources. After keying in your family name, the information is displayed by CJSI in Daitch-Mokotoff soundex order. You will only see codes next to the name. Scroll the screen down to see what these codes represent. They will link to other sites on the

Web that will give you a more detailed description of the source and how to access the information (an Internet database, a reference book, etc). Be sure to research all spelling variants of your surname that are in the CJSI.

Family Tree of the Jewish People

The final Internet database worth searching if you are just starting your research is the Family Tree of the Jewish People at <http://www.jewishgen.org/gedcom>. This is a database of family trees submitted by Jewish genealogists. It contains more than one million individuals. Members of your family may already be on another researcher's family tree, and this database will link you up with the researcher. If you are searching for a common surname, be sure to include a given name or town to limit the scope of the hits.

JewishGen Discussion Group

If you had a problem in your research that you think could be answered by some other Jewish genealogist, wouldn't it be advantageous if there was a way of communicating with all Jewish genealogists at the same time in the hope that one of them could help solve your problem? The JewishGen Discussion Group is such a forum. Internet discussion groups (also known as mailing lists or bulletin boards) are e-mail lists of persons with a common interest. You can post a message that will be read by all persons subscribing to the list. The JewishGen Discussion Group has an estimated 5,000 subscribers; a message you post to this group could be read by all 5,000. Each day some 50 messages are posted in a variety of categories: queries, responses to queries, meeting announcements, new resource discoveries, success stories, tips, etc.

How to become a subscriber and how to post messages to the JewishGen Discussion Group can be found at <http://www.jewishgen.org/JewishGen/DiscussionGroup.htm>.

Periodically Check These Sources

Check these databases every few months. There is information being added constantly. Participate in these databases. Add your surnames and ancestral towns to the JewishGen Family Finder. Once you have computerized your family tree, submit it to the Family Tree of the Jewish People. Subscribe to the JewishGen Discussion Group, and periodically search the recent additions to its archives just in case you missed a posting that might be of interest to you.

Organized Jewish Genealogy

Jewish genealogy is highly organized. There are Jewish Genealogical Societies (JGSs) worldwide under an umbrella group: the International Association of Jewish Genealogical Societies (IAJGS). Since 1982, annual conferences have been held in different cities each year. The New York conference in 1999 attracted more than 1,300 attendees from countries throughout the world. There is an Internet presence for Jewish genealogy called JewishGen that includes a discussion group, databases, infofiles, and other resources.

Jewish Genealogical Societies (JGSs)

There are more than 75 Jewish Genealogical Societies worldwide. They are located in 50 cities in Argentina, Australia, Belgium, Brazil, Canada, France, Germany, Great Britain, Israel, Netherlands, Russia, South Africa, Sweden, Switzerland, and the United States. These societies typically hold meetings once a month throughout the year. There usually is a lecture or discussion session on a genealogy topic at each meeting, and members can discuss research problems and exchange information. Most societies publish a newsletter that provides additional information about genealogical research. Many hold beginners workshops.

The societies are all part of an umbrella group, the International Association of Jewish Genealogical Societies, that acts to represent the Jewish genealogical community to the outside world and to promote interest in Jewish family history research in general.

If a society exists in your area, join it. For the address of the JGS nearest you:

- Internet: <http://www.jewishgen.org/ajgs/ajgs-jgss.html>
- Mail: IAJGS does not have offices, and the postal address changes often as different officers are elected. It is recommended that you use the Internet to locate a society.
- Print: A complete list of societies is copied from the Internet site noted above and published annually in the spring issue of *Avotaynu: The International Review of Jewish Genealogy.*

Special Interest Groups (SIGs)

Special Interest Groups (SIGs) are Jewish genealogical groups organized by geographic area of ancestry or special interest topic. Examples are the Romanian SIG and the Sefard SIG. Because members are located throughout the world, regular meetings are not held; the principal method of communication is through the newsletter of the SIG and/or discussion groups on the Internet. To subscribe to the discussion group, go on the Web to <http://www.jewishgen.org/listserv/sigs.htm> and follow the instructions. Contact information about each SIG is located at the JewishGen website and is also published in the spring issue of *Avotaynu* each year.

Examples of current SIGS include:

By town: Bereza, Bobruisk, Ciechanow, Keidan, Nesvizh, Odessa

By country: Denmark, Germany, Hungary, Latvia, Lithuania, Poland, Romania

By region: Courland, Galicia, Grodno guberniya, Kielce and Radom guberniyas, Latin America, Southern Africa, Suwalk & Lomza guberniyas, Volhynia

Other: Yizkor Book Project, Sefard

JewishGen

If you have access to the Internet, you have access to one of the most important resources of Jewish genealogy: JewishGen, located at <http://www.jewishgen.org>. JewishGen is the brainchild of Susan E. King of Houston, Texas, and the product of hundreds of volunteers who moderate discussion groups, create databases, establish educational programs, and maintain this vast web site.

It is a U.S. non-profit tax exempt organization staffed entirely by volunteers. All its resources are free, but it relies heavily on contributions for ongoing maintenance and continued growth. Contributions (recommended minimum $25.00) are tax deductible to individuals who pay U.S. income tax.

Visiting the home page of JewishGen links you to the subcategories of information available at the site. The major components of JewishGen are described below.

Discussion Groups. The primary discussion group is the JewishGen Discussion Group, a bulletin board where some 50 messages are posted every day. These messages are sent to the more than 5,000 subscribers, who, in turn, respond to the inquiries. Their responses are posted to the Discussion Group. More detailed information about this resource is described in the "Jump-Starting Using the Internet" section of this book. There is a Discussion Group archives that contains every message posted to the Group since 1993. A full-text search engine associated with this archives permits you to search through the years; it locates every message containing the keywords you supply. Search for your surname, and it will locate it in any of the thousands of messages. Key in a town name, and it will find the messages that include the town name.

Many SIGs have their own Discussion Group that is devoted to inquiries and information about their particular interest. For example, there is a Belarus Discussion Group that posts about 10–20 messages a day about research in that country.

Research. JewishGen is the host of numerous databases. The *JewishGen Family Finder* discussed elsewhere in this book is a database of ancestral surnames and towns being researched by more than 30,000 Jewish genealogists throughout the world. *JewishGen ShtetlSeeker* is a database of every town (more than 500,000) in Central and Eastern Europe showing the latitude and longitude for the town as well as a map of the area. The *Family Tree of the Jewish People* is a database of family trees submitted by users of JewishGen (discussed in detail elsewhere in this book). *Jewish Records Indexing—Poland* is an index to more than 500,000 birth, marriage, and death records from 19th-century Poland. *All Lithuania Database* includes information about Lithuanian ancestors from numerous sources. As of August 1999, some 35 other databases were named on the Database page of JewishGen.

InfoFiles. Genealogists throughout the world have submitted files of information (InfoFiles) on a variety of subjects. There are so many files that they are sub-categorized at the JewishGen site into Basics, Books & Periodicals, Cemeteries, Genealogical Techniques, Genealogists, Genetics, Holocaust, Immigration/Emigration, Internet Sources, JewishGen Sources, Libraries & Archives, Military, Miscellaneous, LDS (Mormon) Resources, Names, Postal Matters, Preservation, Seminars, Sephardim, Social Security, Special Interest Groups, Translation/Transliteration, Travel, Vital Records. They are also categorized by country. There are also a small number of datafiles on very specific subjects. One is a list of Jewish passengers on the *Titanic*. To date, there are more than 200 InfoFiles on JewishGen.

Projects: There are a host of projects under the JewishGen umbrella that you might find useful in your research, and the list is growing.

Family Database: Jewish family web sites. Here you can find links to web sites created by Jewish genealogists that provide information about their families.

Holocaust Global Registry: For Holocaust survivors, for survivors searching for family members, and for child survivors who are searching for clues to their identity.

JewishGen ShtetLinks: Web pages devoted to individual communities.

JewishGen ShtetlSchleppers: Information on planned trips to your ancestral town.

JewishGen Yizkor Book Project: A project to facilitate access to yizkor books (Holocaust memorial books) and their contents. Included are databases, translations of portions of yizkor books, infofiles, a discussion group, and links to other sites of interest to this group.

Meetings Database: Provides a list of meetings of interest to JewishGeners.

Online Worldwide Burial Registry: Contains information about Jewish cemeteries throughout the world plus a database of individual burials.

Publication Database: Identifies publications of interest to Jewish genealogical researchers.

TraveLink Database: Descriptions and pictures of trips taken by other researchers to their ancestral towns.

Tools. There are handy tools that will:

- convert a Hebrew date to the secular calendar and vice versa
- display the dates of all Jewish holidays for any year
- compute the distance between two coordinates on the earth in either miles or kilometers
- give you the Daitch-Mokotoff Soundex Code for any word (typically a surname or town name).

Links. There are numerous links to sites outside the JewishGen environment that contain information of possible use in your research.

Publications and Books

Avotaynu: The International Review of Jewish Genealogy

The principal magazine of Jewish genealogy is *Avotaynu: The International Review of Jewish Genealogy*. It was founded in 1985 by Gary Mokotoff of Northvale, New Jersey, and Sallyann Amdur Sack of Bethesda, Maryland. A quarterly publication, it contains articles covering the full spectrum of interest to Jewish genealogists: feature articles, new resources, book reviews, human interest stories, and others. Each issue is at least 68 pages. To date, *Avotaynu* has published some 1,500 articles. A subject index to these articles is on the Internet at <http://www.avotaynu.com/indexsum.htm>. The index is also available in printed form by writing to the publisher. All back issues of the publication (1985–96) are available on CD-ROM with a full-word search engine. An update through 1999 is planned for Spring 2000.

Contributing editors from 15 countries throughout the world regularly gather important information that appears in its issues. The editors continually scour major Jewish genealogical repositories such as American Jewish Archives, American Jewish Historical Society, Central Archives for the History of the Jewish People, LDS (Mormon) Family History Library, Leo Baeck Institute, Search Bureau for Missing Relatives, U.S. Holocaust Memorial Museum, U.S. Library of Congress, U.S. National Archives, Yad Vashem, YIVO Institute, as well as other principal archives and libraries throughout the world.

Authors of articles include not only the most prominent Jewish genealogists, but heads of major archives and libraries throughout the world, scholars, and just plain researchers.

Pioneer Jewish genealogist, Arthur Kurzweil, stated in his book *From Generation to Generation* that "the single most significant development in the field of Jewish genealogy over the past decade has been the appearance of *Avotaynu*...(It) is essential for all Jewish genealogists. You must subscribe to it."

Avotaynu has a Web site at <http://www.avotaynu.com>. Subscription information can be found at <http://www.avotaynu.com/journal.htm>.

Society and SIG Newsletters

Most Jewish Genealogical Societies and some Special Interest Groups publish newsletters. They typically contain announcements of meetings, reviews of lectures at previous meetings, discoveries by members, and other relevant articles. They vary in size from a few stapled pages to multi-page magazines that contain feature articles, extracts and indexes of records, news announcements, and society activities.

Books

There are numerous books available to assist you in your research. One publisher, Avotaynu, Inc., focuses specifically on books for Jewish genealogy and has published more than 20 books in the past eight years. A list of some 50 books of interest to Jewish genealogists appears in Appendix A. If your local library does not have a specific book, ask them if they can get it on interlibrary loan. Most of the books are in print and, therefore, can be purchased if you wish to develop a genealogy library. Avotaynu publishes a semi-annual catalog that includes most of the books mentioned. To get a copy of the catalog, contact the company.

Avotaynu, Inc.
155 N. Washington Ave.
Bergenfield, NJ 07621
Phone: 1-800-AVOTAYNU (286-8296)
Fax: (201) 387-2855
E-mail: info@avotaynu.com
Web: http://avotaynu.com

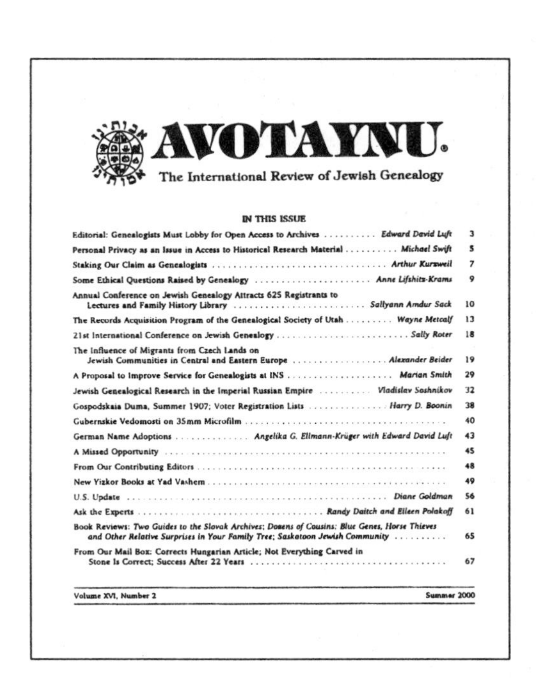
AVOTAYNU®
The International Review of Jewish Genealogy

IN THIS ISSUE

Volume XVI, Number 2 Summer 2000

Finding Records of Your Ancestors

It is virtually impossible for any person to have lived on this Earth in the past 200 years without leaving some trace of his or her existence. Everyone of us was born; there may be a birth record of the event. Your ancestors were married (at least mine were); there may have been a marriage record. When your ancestors died, there may have been a death certificate. Your ancestors may have voted, owned property, owned a business, joined an organization, notarized a statement, been mugged, or been a mugger. All these events created records.

The great myth of Jewish genealogy is that all the Jewish records in Central and Eastern Europe were destroyed in the Holocaust. Nothing could be further from the truth. While most things Jewish were destroyed, governmental and secular records usually survived; you just have to know how to find them. Described below are some of the most basic classes of records that will provide you with information about your ancestors.

There are certain records that are especially useful for Jewish genealogical research.

• Vital Records. The birth, marriage, and death records of your ancestors

• Naturalization records. The documents created by the process by which your ancestors became citizens of the country to which they immigrated

• Passenger emigration/immigration lists. The passenger lists of the ships on which your ancestors left Europe and arrived in their new country

• Census records. Every country takes a census of its population.

• Special records such as those of the U.S. Social Security Administration, military records, probate records, and others

Vital Records (Births, Marriages, and Deaths)

Today, every government keeps track of its population by demanding that all births, marriages, and deaths be recorded (called, as a group, vital records). This is a recent concept, started in the United States in the 19th century and, in some states, as recently as the early 20th century. Some European countries, such as Poland, started in the beginning of the 19th century. In many parts of today's Germany and Holland recordkeeping began as early as the 16th century, and in Hungary not until the mid-19th century.

Typically, these events were recorded at the civil registration office of the town and kept there for 100 years, after which time they were transferred to the governmental archives system. There is a question of privacy, and often birth records are not available for 75–100 years after the event (for example, except in very few states, you cannot get someone else's birth record), but marriage and death records have much shorter privacy requirements varying considerably by government institution. Before you send away for copies of vital records, determine what privacy rules exist for the documents.

Vital records are important genealogical tools because they are considered primary evidence, that is, documents that were recorded at the time the event took place. Therefore, they are highly accurate and contain valuable information. Birth records [see example on page 54] contain name of child, birth date, name of father, name of mother (often mother's birth name), and may also contain such information as age of parents, occupation of father, number of children in prior births. In some countries, if the parents are not from the town where the birth is recorded, it will name the towns of the parents. Marriage records [see example on page 55] include names of bride, groom, their parents, ages of bride and groom, what town they are from. It may also include other information such as occupation of groom and if any of the parents are deceased. Death records [see example on page 56] show the name and age of the person who died and may include names of relatives.

In the United States, vital records are maintained by the individual states, not by the federal government. For larger cities such as New York and Chicago, they are archived by the city, not the state. There is no nationwide registry of births, marriages, or deaths. The complete listing of addresses and fees for each state is available on the Web at: <http://www.cdc.gov/nchswww/howto/w2w/w2welcom.htm>. The actual forms to be used are in the book *International Vital Records Handbook (New Third Edition)*. Particulars about this book are in Appendix A.

In other countries, archived vital records are maintained by a state archival system that, in larger countries, may also have regional archives. It is best to contact your local Jewish Genealogical Society (or consult InfoFiles on JewishGen) to learn how to contact these state archives. You can write to them in your native language. The response is often in their native language.

Naturalization Records

Today, virtually all Jews live in lands that are different from where their ancestors lived 150 years ago. All governments have a process by which immigrants become naturalized citizens. This process produces documents that can contain a considerable amount of genealogical information.

In the United States, there are three basic types of naturalization documents:

• *Declaration of Intention ("First Papers").* Usually filed soon after immigrant's arrival. It usually contains minimal information such as name of person and current address.

• *Petition for Naturalization ("Final Papers").* [See example on page 57.] Filed after required waiting period (usually five years). These papers contain the most information (although the Declaration of Intention may also include comparable information). Documents after 1906 include the applicant's name; address at time of application; town and country of birth; date of birth; date of arrival in the U.S.; if by ship, the name of the ship; name of spouse; date and birthplace of spouse. If spouse is not a citizen, included will be the identical information about town and country of birth; date of birth; date of arrival in the U.S.; if by ship, the name of the ship. Other information may include date of marriage, names of children and ages and/or dates of birth, names and addresses of witnesses who often are family members.

• *Certificate of Citizenship.* Given to the new citizen to take home, therefore, the document most likely to be in the possession of the family. This does not provide much genealogical information, but does contain the name of the court where the person was naturalized and, therefore, can shorten the search process for the Declaration of Intention and Petition for Naturalization.

Before 1906, U.S. naturalizations could be performed in any court: federal, state, county, or local. There were no uniform procedures; the information contained in these records varies greatly from court to court. There are no centralized indexes to these pre-1906 records—you need to know which court (but see information on indexes, below).

Locating Naturalization Records. In 1906, the U.S. government set up the Immigration and Naturalization Service (INS), who established standard forms and procedures. All naturalization records after September 27, 1906, have duplicate copies filed at the Immigration and Naturalization Service, FOIA/PA Section, Room 5304, 425 Eye Street NW, Washington, DC 20536; (202) 514-1554. Since it can take a year or more to receive a response from the INS, use them as a last resort—try to find the original papers at the courthouse (or the archives that inherited that court's old records) or copies of the records on microfilm as described below. This could be a federal, state, county, or local court.

Most of the federal court indexes and pre-1930 records have been microfilmed and are available through all LDS (Mormon) Family History Centers [see chapter that describes the LDS (Mormon) Family History Library]. For a few regions of the country, comprehensive indexes to pre-1906 federal naturalization records were prepared during the 1930s:

- New England (all 6 states, 1790–1906)
- New York City (all 5 boroughs, 1790–1906)

These card indexes are at the National Archives and are also available on microfilm through all LDS Family History Centers.

LDS has microfilmed naturalization papers (up through 1929) at many county courthouses over the last dozen years. To find them, look in the FHL Locality Catalog under the heading: "[State], [County] — Naturalization and Citizenship."

See Appendix A for a list of books that can assist you with further information on how to access naturalization records.

Passenger Lists

United States Passenger Lists. Lists of passengers arriving at U.S. ports [see example on page 58] have been maintained by the federal government since 1820 and are available to the public on microfilm. U.S. passenger arrival lists generally provide the name, ag
e, and country of origin for each arriving person. Relatively few U.S. lists prior to 1890 show the town or city of origin. From about 1905, the lists provide the specific place of last residence and birthplace; therefore, if your ancestor arrived in the U.S. after 1905 and you do not know his/her place of birth, the passenger arrival manifest is a good source.

Passenger lists are arranged by port, then chronologically by date of arrival. These lists have been microfilmed and are available at the National Archives in Washington; portions are available at the various Regional Archives. All passenger lists and indexes may also be borrowed through all LDS Family History Centers. Indexes to many ports were prepared in the 1930s, but they are not complete—some claim the error rate may be as high as 20 percent. The following chart shows the five major U.S. ports of entry on the Atlantic coast:

Port	**Passengers**	**Lists**	**Indexes**
New York	24.0M	1820–1957	1820–1846, 1897–1948
Boston	2.0M	1820–1943	1848–1891, 1902–1920
Baltimore	1.5M	1820–1948	1820–1952
Philadelphia	1.2M	1800–1945	1800–1948
New Orleans	0.7M	1820–1945	1853–1952

The second column shows the number of passengers, in millions, that arrived at each port between 1820 and 1920. The third column shows for which years there are actual lists; the fourth column, which years there are indexes. Note that for the important immigrant port of New York, there are no indexes for the years 1847–96. There are also lists for several minor ports, as well as the Canadian border. As you can see, the large majority of passengers arrived at New York, and there are large gaps in the indexes, especially for periods of major Jewish immigration.

Because passenger lists are arranged by port and then chronologically, it is important to know when and where your ancestor arrived. This information can usually be found on naturalization papers. The U.S. federal census for 1900, 1910, and 1920 lists the year of immigration, and 1920 lists the year of naturalization.

If you know the exact date and port of arrival, you can order a copy of the ship's passenger list directly from the National Archives. Submit National Archives Form NATF-81, "Order for Copies of Ship Passenger Arrival Records," available from the General Reference Branch, National Archives, 7th and Pennsylvania Avenue NW, Washington, D.C. 20408.

The search is free, but you will be billed $10.00 if you wish to receive a copy of the passenger list. These are large full-size copies, 18" x 24", providing much information, especially for 20th-century immigrants.

The National Archives staff will also search the available indexes, if you provide the passenger's full name, port of entry, and approximate date of arrival. Always be aware that no one can do your genealogy as well as you can—no one else will be as thorough and check alternate spellings of names, broader ranges of dates, etc. It is always best to search the original records yourself. Searching passenger lists and indexes can be a challenging and time-consuming task, but one that pays off in the end. You can find your immigrant ancestor on a ship's manifest if you work at it.

These passenger lists were filled out on board by the ship's purser and checked by customs or immigration authorities upon arrival; thus, the names on these lists are the European, pre-Americanized versions. You must know what your ancestor's name was in Europe. The given name is invariably the person's Yiddish name (Moishe, not Morris; Chaim, not Hyman; Chaia, not Ida), and the surname may be as it was spelled in Polish, Russian, Hungarian, etc. (Mokotow, not Mokotoff; Cukierman, not Zuckerman; Minc, not Mintz).

If you know the name of the ship upon which your ancestor arrived in the United States, you can find the dates of that ship's arrival in the *Morton Allan Directory of European Passenger Steamship Arrivals* (1931, reprinted by Genealogical Publishing Co., 1998). It lists names of vessels arriving by year, steamship company, and date of arrival at the ports of New York, 1890–1930, and of Baltimore, Boston, and Philadelphia, 1904–26. This can help narrow your search.

If your ancestor arrived during a period for which the port is unindexed, you have no choice but to search every list, line by line, for that year.

There are some published indexes to passenger lists; most, however, cover pre-Civil War immigrants. Two published indexes are worth noting. *Germans to America*, (Wilmington, DE: Scholarly Resources, 1988+), covers arrivals of German passengers from January 1850 to May 1891. This ongoing series (60 volumes thus far) is available at major libraries. A published index for Russian immigrants covering czarist Russia (includes Russian-Poland, Lithuania, Belarus, and Ukraine) arrivals has been published. It is titled *Migration from the Russian Empire: Lists of Passengers Arriving at U.S. Ports*, edited by Ira Glazier, (Baltimore: Genealogical Publishing Co., 1995+). The first six volumes contain arrivals for January 1875 to June 1891 and include 300,000 names (of the 2.3 million Russians who arrived 1871–1910). Volumes 7 and 8 are anticipated by the end of 1999. They will likely cover 1892–93.

Canadian Passenger Lists: The National Archives of Canada (395 Wellington St., Ottawa K1A 0N3 Canada) has microfilm copies of passenger manifests for ships arriving at six Canadian ports, including Quebec (from 1865) and Halifax (from 1881) up to 1935. These lists are arranged chronologically; there is no name index. For details see the National Archives of Canada site: <http://www.archives.ca>. Records after 1936 are subject to restrictions of the Privacy Act. Inquiries on these later records may be addressed to: Query Response Centre, Citizenship and Immigration, 300 Slater Street, Ottawa, Ontario K1A 1L1 Canada. (613) 957-7667.

The U.S. government maintained lists of people crossing the border from Canada. These Canadian Border Crossing lists, also known as the "St. Albans Lists," cover 1895–1954. They contain information similar to ship passenger manifests and are indexed. The lists and indexes are available at the U.S. National Archives in Washington, several of the Regional Branches, and at the LDS (Mormon) Family History Libraries.

Hamburg Emigration Lists: Many European ports maintained emigration lists. The most complete and accessible are for the port of Hamburg, Germany, where lists of emigrating passengers were maintained for 1850–1934. About 40% of Eastern European Jewish immigrants (Polish, Russian, Hungarian, etc.) left via Hamburg. These lists contain the emigrant's town of origin. They are indexed by year and first letter of each passenger's surname, so some searching is required. The lists and indexes have been microfilmed and are available through LDS Family History Centers.

Census Records

Most countries take censuses of their population, typically every ten years. The United States takes a census every ten years during the year that ends with the digit 0 [see example on page 60]. Canada and Great Britain take censuses every ten years on the year that ends with the digit 1. Information in a census is considered confidential for a period of time. In the U.S., census data is not made public for 72 years; in Canada and Great Britain after 100 years. This means the most recently available U.S. census is 1920. In 2002, the 1930 census will be released. The records of the 1890 U.S. census were destroyed in a fire; no copies survived.

Most census records have been indexed:

- 1790–1870: Privately compiled, published indexes for most states.
- 1880: Partial index for all states: includes only households with children age 10 and under. Soundex index for each state.
- 1890: More than 99.99% of census records destroyed in a fire.
- 1900: Complete soundex index for each state.
- 1910: Soundex index for only 21 states (most in the south and west): AL, AR, CA, FL, GA, IL, KS, KY, LA, MI, MS, MO, NC, OH, OK, PA, SC, TN, TX, VA, WV.
- 1920: Complete soundex index for each state.

Censuses can provide valuable information about a household. They list every person (in the U.S. since 1850) showing name, age, place of birth (state or country), occupation, and relationship to the head of household. Even the name can provide useful information because immigrant ancestors tended to give their children Yiddish given names; these appear on censuses during their early years. Thus, you determine Aunt Sally was born Sadie and Uncle Herman was named Chaim.

Certain censuses have useful information for Jewish genealogists whose ancestors came during the massive wave of immigration from 1881–1924. The 1900 census asked of non-native born people what year they arrived in the U.S. This was also asked in the 1910 census. The 1920 census also asked in what year the person became a citizen. If not a citizen, was citizenship applied for. This can be useful information if you do not know what year an immigrant ancestor arrived in the United States.

Other Records

To reiterate. It is virtually impossible for any person to have lived on this Earth during the past 200 years without leaving some trace of his or her existence. Your ancestors may have voted, owned property, owned a business, joined an organization, notarized a statement, been mugged, or been a mugger. All these events created records.

Cemeteries. Your friends may think you ghoulish, but now that you have entered the wonderful world of genealogy, one of your great desires will be to visit cemeteries. A relative recently praised the work of our family's genealogist but noted, "She is doing a great job, but she's a little *meshuggah* (crazy). She takes pictures of tombstones."

Cemeteries and tombstones contain valuable information about a particular family member [see example on page 65]. A traditional tombstone gives the name of the deceased, Hebrew name, Hebrew name of his/her father, date of death, and either birth date or, more normally, age at time of death. The inscription "Beloved brother, father, and grandfather" informs you the deceased had at least one sibling, was married, was likely predeceased by his wife (beloved husband is missing), had at least one child who was married, and had at least one grandchild.

There may be additional information. If born into the Cohanic or Levitic priestly classes, it will be stated on a tombstone. Rabbis are given an extra word or two preceding a name.

The treasure does not end at the gravesite. The cemetery's office records may include name of next of kin; the person paying for the upkeep of the plot. This can be a link to living relatives previously unknown to you.

City Directories and Telephone Books. Telephone books and their precursors, city directories, may place your ancestor at a specific address at a specific time. This can be valuable in locating their census record in those years that are unindexed. Many old city directories show occupation of the individual. Going through city directories chronologically can give an estimated year of death of the father of a household by noting the first year his name disappears from a city directory and is replaced by the wife's name.

Compiled Genealogies. Your genealogy may be done already ... well, at least a portion of it. There are books of family trees (called compiled genealogies) mostly of distinguished Jewish families. Some are listed in Appendix A.

Military Records. Many men, and some women, served in the armed forces. These records are confidential, unless you can prove the person is deceased. One set of records in the public domain is the World War I draft records. They have been microfilmed by the LDS Family History Library.

Newspaper Obituaries. Obituaries usually include the names of all close kin. They also can include the name of the funeral parlor and place of interment. Both the funeral director and cemetery may have information of value to you. For example, if you are trying to locate kin to a distant ancestor, the cemetery will have the name and address of the person paying for care of the grave. Some cemeteries will not disclose this information, but may be willing to forward a letter to these individuals.

Probate Records. When a person dies and there is a will, the will must go through a legal process called probate. These records are public documents, and you can get copies of them. Since they provide names of people who will inherit the estate, they often include, in addition to the names of the heirs, their addresses at the time the will was filed for probate and their relationship to the person making the will. Wills and the probation proceedings are filed in probate courts. Based on personal experience, these seem to be the hardest records to get. Often the clerks in the probate courts consider genealogists unwanted inquirers, and rules are made to discourage these kinds of inquiries. For example, you can go to a court and be told to come back in two days (to two weeks) to retrieve the records.

Social Security Death Index. There is one unusual Internet resource that is worth isolating and describing: the Social Security Death Index (SSDI) [see example on page 64]. This database is a list of every person who died in the United States since 1960 for whom there was a Social Security death claim since 1962, some 60 million people. It comes closest to a U.S. national death index. SSDI can also be searched on the Web: <http://www.ancestry.com/ssdi/advanced.htm> and other Internet sites. It is also available at nearly all LDS Family History Centers, many large libraries, and can be purchased from a number of genealogy vendors.

Most SSDI entries will tell you the date of birth and death and zip code of last residence. From this information you can then write to the state for a death certificate. The Internet sites also provide the Social Security number and a form letter to be used to send for a copy of the person's original Social Security application (Form SS-5). Write to: Freedom of Information Officer, 4H8 Annex Building, 6401 Security Blvd., Baltimore, MD 21235. The cost for a copy of the SS-5 form is $7.00. The original application contains the date and place of birth, as well as both parents' full names as provided by the applicant.

Synagogue Records. A very poor source of information. They rarely have any information other than names/addresses of past and current members. Unlike Christian churches, which have been instructed to keep records of baptisms, marriages, and deaths since the 16th century, it has never been the function of synagogues to maintain such records.

Voter Registration Records. This can be a useful source to determine the court in which an immigrant was naturalized. In order to vote, you had to demonstrate you were a citizen. If you were born in the U.S., your birth certificate was proof. If you were born outside the U.S., you presented your citizenship certificate. The information from the certificate, including the court where naturalized, was written into the voter's record. Unfortunately, voter registration records are not very high on an archivist's retention list; therefore, many governments destroy them after a number of years of disuse. Contact the local Board of Elections to determine where old lists are kept and how old the records are.

Libraries, Archives And Historical Societies

Public Libraries

One of the most valuable resources for your genealogical research is your local library—no matter how small it is. If you are interested in using a book and it is not available at your local library, ask the librarian whether it can be obtained through interlibrary loan. Libraries tend to operate on two levels in the interlibrary loan system. They will check on their computer system (in many libraries you can check it yourself) to see if the book you want is at another local library. If so, you can go there or borrow it through the interlibrary loan system. All libraries are part of a national interlibrary loan system and can get you virtually any book that is part of the system, no matter which library in the country has it. If necessary, they can borrow it from the Library of Congress. It works. Gary Mokotoff lives in a town of 5,000 people with a very small municipal library. He once borrowed, on interlibrary loan, a book about the Jews of the Canary Islands. The librarian located the book at a university library about 40 miles away. When he received the book, he observed that it had not been taken out of the university library in 38 years!

Not every book is available through interlibrary loan. Rare books, for example yizkor books, may not be part of the system. Often reference works, which may be on demand at the lending library, may be reserved for their own patrons.

University Libraries

Is there a college or university in your area? These institutions tend to have larger libraries than municipal libraries and the collections are of a more scholarly nature.

Library of Congress

The Library of Congress (LOC) is the library of the U.S. government. It is the largest library in the world, with more than 115 million items on approximately 530 miles of bookshelves. The collections include some 17 million books, 2 million recordings, 12 million photographs, 4 million maps, and 50 million manuscripts. Every book ever copyrighted in the U.S. is part of their collection. If your local library does not have a book and they claim they cannot locate it in their own interlibrary loan system, ask them to get the book from the Library of Congress. LOC's Geography and Map Division holds the world's largest collection of cartographic materials, 4.6 million items. This includes numerous maps of Central and Eastern Europe, many dating back to the 18th or 19th century. Explore the numerous resources described at their Internet site: <http://www.loc.gov>. An online catalog is included.

LDS (Mormon) Family History Library

Would you believe that one of the best resources for Jewish genealogy is associated with a church? The Church of Jesus Christ of Latter-day Saints (LDS), also known as the Mormon Church, operates the Family History Library (FHL), the largest genealogical library in the world. Located in Salt Lake City, Utah, their collection contains more than 2,000,000 reels of microfilm, 700,000 microfiche, and 280,000 books. Some are Jewish records; many are secular records of your ancestors, including records of their birth, marriage, and death.

You don't have to go to Utah to access these records. The Church operates more than 3,400 Family History Centers (FHCs) in 64 countries worldwide. At your request, records on microfilm can be sent from Salt Lake City to any Family History Center for a small fee to cover the cost of postage. The books and microfiche collections are not available to FHCs. To find a Family History Center near you, look in the Yellow Pages under "Churches" for the local Church of Jesus Christ of Latter-day Saints. Call them and ask for the FHC hours. Alternately, a list of FHCs is on the Internet at <http://familysearch.com/Search/Searchfhc2.asp>.

The Mormons' interest in genealogy stems from their religious beliefs. Theirs is a young religion, founded in the 1820s in New York State. Mormons have a religious obligation to determine who their ancestors were and bring (baptize) them into the faith. They have extended this practice to include all persons, independent of whether or not they are ancestors.

Consequently, the Church has made a systematic effort to microfilm records of genealogical value from all over the world, including Jewish records. They have microfilmed an extensive collection of 19th-century Jewish vital records from Poland, Germany, and Hungary. A catalog of these records (over 5,000 microfilm reels) is available on the Internet at the LDS site <http://www.familysearch.org>. A description of how to use this site is described below in "How to Search the Family History Library Catalog." A downloadable version of the Polish holdings is available at <http://www.jewishgen.org/JRI-PL/jri-lds.htm>.

Nearly all U.S. National Archives microfilms (federal census, passenger lists, naturalization records, military records); many U.S. state, county, and city records; as well as records from nearly every country on earth, are available, also.

In 1995, the Church signed an agreement with leaders of major Jewish organizations to no longer posthumously baptize Jews. In reality, few deceased Jews had been posthumously baptized to that date. The agreement was the result of a single incident in which a group of overzealous Mormons had baptized some 360,000 Jews murdered in the Holocaust. The Mormons proselytize, but it is Church policy not to mix genealogy with religion, and acts of proselytizing at Family History Centers are extremely rare. With the growing interest in family history among Jews, we are heavy users of the Mormon facilities.

How to Search the Family History Library Catalog

To determine whether there are records of your ancestral town in the FHL collection, it is necessary to use their Family History Library catalog, an index of the more than two million rolls of microfilm, hundreds of thousands of books, and other materials available at the Family History Library in Salt Lake City. The catalog is available on CD-ROM or microfiche at any FHC, and the volunteers at the center will show you how to use it.

To use the Internet version, go to the catalog on the Web at <http://www.familysearch.org>. At the home page, click the tab marked "Custom Search." On the next page, click the link to the Family History Library Catalog. Finally, click the button to do a Place Search. You are now at the page where you can initiate searches by town. Bookmark this page to avoid the three-step process just described the next time you want to use the catalog. Key in the town name and follow the instructions on how to use the catalog.

Records in the FHL catalog are defined at three levels: town, province or county, and country. All three must be searched separately in order to determine what the Family History Library holds. For example, a book on Jewish cemeteries of Poland may include information about the cemetery in your ancestral town. It will not, however, appear in the catalog under the name of a specific ancestral town; rather, it will appear under the country name.

Family History Source Guides

Visitors to the Family History Library are familiar with the multitude of pamphlets published to assist in genealogical research. Research outlines for each state in the United States, every province of Canada, and many countries are available. Topics include such items as a source guide of 300 most common words to be found on Polish vital records and a guide on how to use Hamburg passenger lists.

These are all available at the Internet site and can be printed on your computer's printer.

Archives and Historical Societies

Archives are the permanent repositories of the historical records of a government, institution, or individual. Records that are in current use remain with the government department, institution, or individual for a specific number of years after which they are either destroyed or kept permanently in an archives.

U.S. National Archives and Records Administration (NARA). This institution, the permanent repository of the historical records of all U.S. government departments, is located in Washington, D.C., and has 13 regional archives throughout the nation. Consequently, it is the primary source for U.S. federal census records, passenger lists, military records, and some naturalization records. The Archives is located at 8th and Pennsylvania Ave. N.W., Washington, DC 20408. Phone: (202) 501-5400. The best overview is the book *Guide to Genealogical Research in the National Archives*. A description of NARA's genealogical resources is on the Internet at <http://www.nara.gov/genealogy/>. NARA sells some publications that are useful for genealogical research. They are described in the free booklet *Aids for Genealogical Research* (29 pages), available from: Product Sales Staff (NWPS), National Archives, 700 Pennsylvania Ave. NW, Room G-7, Washington DC, 20408-0001. Phone: (800) 234-8861. Fax: (202) 501-7170. The National Archives and its branches are open to the public and available for use free of charge. The addresses of the regional archives can be found at <http://www.nara.gov/nara/gotonara.html>. Microfilms are in open cabinets, and the staff is helpful and knowledgeable. Note that nearly all National Archives microfilms are also available through all LDS (Mormon) Family History Centers.

State, County, and Municipal Archives. Each state has its own archival system for permanent historical records. They contain the older birth, marriage, and death records; state censuses; and probate records. *Genealogist's Address Book* described in Appendix A contains the addresses and telephone numbers of most of these facilities. Many of these repositories have Internet sites that describe their holdings and how to access them. Use a search engine such as <http://www.yahoo.com> to locate their web site. Searching Yahoo with the words "Illinois State Archives" immediately found the location of that archives on the Internet.

Historical Societies. Historical societies are institutions that permanently preserve the history of some region, be it a town, county, state, or special interest.

Jewish Archives and Libraries. Some archives that focus on Jewish material are worth noting; all include a library. These archives contain records of Jewish organizations. If your ancestor was a member of, or was served by, a particular Jewish organization, you may be able to find information about this person at these archives. Visit their respective web sites for additional information regarding hours of operation, genealogical inquiries, etc.

American Jewish Archives (AJA). The Jacob Rader Marcus Center of the American Jewish Archives is located at 3101 Clifton Ave., Cincinnati, OH 45220. Phone: (513) 221-1875. E-mail: aja@huc.edu. Web site: <http://www.huc.edu/aja>. Their web site has a section covering genealogical inquiries. This archives, as well as the American Jewish Historical Society, is known for their collection of the early Jewish presence in the U.S. They are also the archives for a number of institutions such as the World Jewish Congress (WJC). The WJC was very active in identifying and relocating Holocaust survivors; therefore, AJA has Holocaust survivor lists that are part of the WJC collection.

American Jewish Historical Society. Currently located in Waltham, Massachusetts, but soon to move to the Center for Jewish History, 15 W. 16 St., New York, NY 10011. The Society, a major repository of records of the Jewish presence in the Western Hemisphere, hopes to reopen in January 2000. Their New York phone number is (212) 294-6160. Check their web site at <http://www.ajhs.org> for the status of their move to their new facilities.

Leo Baeck Institute. Currently located at 129 W. 73 St., New York, NY 10021, the Institute also plans to move to the Center for Jewish History. Phone: (212) 744-6400. Web site: <http://www.users.interport.net/~lbi1/>. The library and archives offers the most comprehensive documentation for the study of the history of German-speaking Jewry. There are locations in London and Jerusalem.

YIVO Institute for Jewish Research. The first tenant of the new Center for Jewish History, 15 W. 16 St., New York, NY 10011. Phone: (212) 246-6080. Web site: <http://www.baruch.cuny.edu/yivo/>. This, the largest library and archives of Eastern European Jewry, was founded in Vilnius (Vilna), Lithuania, in 1925. Much of its pre-Holocaust holdings were rescued. Its yizkor (Holocaust memorial) book collection is second only to Yad Vashem in Jerusalem.

Holocaust Research

Every family with roots in Central and Eastern Europe has family members who were murdered in the Holocaust. If your family left that part of the world many years ago and your ancestors were safe elsewhere, you haven't completed your family tree. As you go back in time and discover ancestors, you will also come forward in time documenting the brothers and sisters of these ancestors and their descendants. Only then will you come to know how your family was affected by the Holocaust.

Most of your family members murdered in the Holocaust died without a tombstone or gravesite to mark their passing. In some cases, the fact that they ever existed has been eradicated by acts of war or the deliberate acts of the Nazis and their collaborators. Placing them on your family tree documents that they once lived; it is a permanent memorial to them.

There is a definitive book on Holocaust research, *How to Document Victims and Locate Survivors of the Holocaust* (Teaneck, New Jersey: Avotaynu, 1996). It provides a step-by-step procedure on how to locate records of victims and survivors in your family. Key portions of the book are available on the Internet at <http://www.avotaynu.com/Holocaust/>.

To determine the fate of family members who were caught up in the Holocaust, the above-named book provides a checklist of items to consider. Particulars about these resources are described in the book or at the Internet site.

• If you are not familiar with the circumstances surrounding the fate of the Jews of the town where the survivors and/or victims lived before the Holocaust, read a book on the history of the Holocaust that describes these events. Two such books are *Ghetto Anthology* and *Encyclopedia of the Holocaust.*

• Determine if there is a yizkor book for the town in which the people of interest lived. Yizkor books are Holocaust memorial books that document and remember the towns and townspeople destroyed in the Holocaust. To date, more than one thousand such works have been published, each for an individual town or region. They include articles written by survivors and often provide a great deal of information about specific individuals from the town, perhaps members of your family. Consult the book to see if there is mention of the individuals or family names you are researching. The most complete list of towns with yizkor books published about them can be found on the Internet at <http:www.JewishGen.org/yizkor/database.html>.

• If the person(s) is a Holocaust victim and his fate is not known, write to the Hall of Names at Yad Vashem[2] to see if a Page of Testimony has been submitted for that individual. A description of Pages of Testimony and the procedure to acquire these documents are described in the book or at the book's Internet site, <http://www.avotaynu.com/Holocaust/>.

• Check the records of the International Tracing Service for information about survivors and victims, either by writing to them using the Foreign Inquiry Location Service of the American Red Cross or by consulting the microfilm copy at Yad Vashem in person. Information on how to access these institutions can be found in the book or at the book's Internet site.

• If searching for a survivor, write a letter to the organizations in various countries that maintain lists of survivors or that assisted survivors in relocating after World War II. A list of such organizations can be found at the book site: <http://www.avotaynu.com/Holocaust/>.

• Contact a local Holocaust Resource Center for information about the latest resources found for Holocaust research. If the local facility does not have a book or record known to be available elsewhere, ask them to secure a copy of the information for their permanent collection or as a loan copy. New acquisitions are constantly being made, and resource sites regularly share their information. A complete list can be found at <http://www.ushmm.org/organizations/list.html>.

• Consider asking for help from a Jewish Genealogical Society. Their members are researching their families' histories. Because the Holocaust has had such a profound effect on contemporary Jewish families, members have developed expertise in Holocaust research. Jewish Genealogical Societies are discussed elsewhere in this book.

• If you have the option of either going to or writing to a major resource center, go there in person. Many research sites are very conscientious about processing mail inquiries, but the recipient of your request can devote only a limited amount of time to your inquiry. If you go to the facility, you can spend the hours necessary to peruse secondary sources of information. Browse the catalog of the holdings of the facility.

---

[2]Yad Vashem Holocaust Martyrs' and Heroes' Remembrance Authority, located in Jerusalem, was established and instructed by Israeli Law in 1953, to commemorate the six million Jews murdered in the Holocaust and the communities in which they lived. It has the largest and the most comprehensive archive and information repositories on the Holocaust, housing more than 50 million pages of documents and hundreds of thousands of photographs and films. Over 75,000 titles and periodicals comprise the most significant library on Holocaust research in the world.

See if there is information about any of the towns of interest. Some references may include details about specific individuals that are not obvious in the catalog description of the work. Cataloging is an imperfect process that, to a certain extent, relies on the judgment of the cataloger. An example is Record Group RG-15.019M at the U.S. Holocaust Research Institute. Its description is "Court inquiries about executions and graves in districts, provinces, camps, and ghettos"—19 microfilm reels. Its purpose is to document Nazi atrocities in Poland. The names of victims are given in many cases.

When writing to a research facility about a specific individual or family, give as much information as possible—but be concise. Limit your letter to facts about the individual, including exact name, date of birth (even if year only or approximate year), place of birth, names of immediate family members, and last known residence address. Any information that can uniquely identify the individual from the thousands, if not millions, of pieces of information at the research site is important. Inadequate information will prompt a rejection of your request, which will only delay your research. Picture yourself at the facility trying to do the research. Could you find the information requested given the information you supplied?

Da No. 17114 - Sch.J.Pole
Date 1.12.50/SL
Name MOKOTOW, Berek File GCC3/62/IL/4
BD 11.3.92 BP Warschau Nat Polish-Jew.
Next of Kin
Source of Information Orig.Dachau Entry Register
Last kn. Location Date
CC/Prison Dachau Arr. 3.9.40 from Sachsenhausen
Transf. on to
Died on 15.1.41 ? in CC Dachau
Cause of death
Buried on in
Grave D.C. No.
Remarks home address:Frankfurt a.M., Schichaustr.4

***International Tracing Service**: ITS maintains more than 45 million index cards that reference documents in their collection about individuals caught up in the Holocaust: victims and survivors. This index card documents the death of Berek Mokotow who died in Dachau.*

Special Problem: Finding Your Ancestral Town

Many beginning genealogists do not know their ancestral town. Family lore sometimes at best indicates they came from Russia, or Austria, or Lithuania. There is also a risk that family legend says they came from Vilna or Minsk, but evidence eventually uncovers that this meant Vilna guberniya (province) or Minsk guberniya. This is similar to Americans who claim they are from New York. Do they mean New York City or New York State?

To further confound the situation, if family legend says you came from a particular country, what is meant is the country as it existed when they came to the United States. Today's Poland, at the turn of the 20th century, was not an independent country, but consisted of portions of the Russian, German, and Austro-Hungarian Empires. The area at the turn of the century that was called Poland then, today is partially in Poland, Lithuania, Belarus, and Ukraine.

If you do not know your ancestral town, it is a brick wall that must be circumvented, because you will not be able to go back in time to locate records of your ancestors without this vital piece of information.

There are some primary sources of information that will identify your ancestral town.

Naturalization Records

Prior to becoming a citizen, your ancestor filled out an application to become a citizen called a "Declaration of Intention" (also known as "First Papers"). The information also appears on the Petition for Naturalization (also known as "Final Papers"). One question asked of applicants was, "Where were you born?" That is the good news. The bad news is that the clerk preparing the document invariably wrote down what he heard as the name of the town. With a thick Yiddish accent, town names can be distorted. The good news is there is a gazetteer of Central and Eastern Europe, *Where Once We Walked* (Teaneck, N.J.: Avotaynu, 1991), that has a soundex index (an index by how a word sounds rather than how it is spelled) of the 35,000 town names in the book. Take the town name as it appears on the naturalization papers, soundex the name, and look it up in the soundex index of the book. From the choices in the soundex index, determine which is your town.

If your family memorabilia includes the Certificate of Citizenship of your ancestor, the document will state the court in which your ancestor was naturalized. Contact the court to determine where the naturalization documents are now kept. Many of these naturalizations have been microfilmed by the LDS (Mormon) Family History Library (see chapter on this facility).

Passenger Arrival Records

Since the early part of the 19th century, when a ship came to the United States, it was required that a list of passengers on the ship be submitted to the authorities. These lists exist on microfilm at the U.S. National Archives. Other major resource centers, such as the LDS (Mormon) Family History Library, have copies. Passenger arrival lists, after 1893, contain a column for "Last Residence," which might be town, province, or country, depending upon the ship. Lists after 1906 added birthplace, both city and country. If your ancestor came before 1893, passenger arrival lists will be of little use to you since they only show country of origin. Note, however, that emigrations lists, notably those of the port of Hamburg, Germany (described below), do show town of origin.

There is an advantage to using passenger arrival records as a research source compared to naturalization records; the arrival records likely had the town name spelled correctly. That is the good news. The bad news is that the name of the town is the name as it existed at the time of arrival. Due to the political changes in Eastern Europe during the past 100 years, town names changed, country names changed, and boundaries changed. Again, the valuable source is *Where Once We Walked*, which has some 15,000 alternate names for towns. Look in this gazetteer to determine the current name of the town.

The most important lists to Jewish genealogists are for the Port of New York, the so-called "Ellis Island" lists, because the majority of Jewish immigrants from Europe came through Ellis Island. If your ancestor came to the United States through Ellis Island after 1896, you do not have to know the name of the ship and the exact date of arrival. For the time period 1897–1948, the lists are fully indexed in three sections: 1897–1902 in alphabetical order; 1903–43, in American Soundex order; 1944–1948 in American Soundex order.

Lists also exist for other ports including Baltimore, Boston, Galveston, New Orleans, Philadelphia, San Francisco, and Savannah.

Both the lists and the indexes are available at the National Archives in Washington, D.C.; selected regional branches of the National Archives; and some major libraries, including the LDS (Mormon) Family History Library.

Hamburg Emigration Lists

Many ports in Europe created emigration lists of people leaving their ports. Few lists have survived and fewer are easily accessible to the public. One port where the lists survived and are accessible is Hamburg, Germany. If your ancestors came before 1896 or you cannot find naturalization records, try the Hamburg Emigration Lists. Many Central and Eastern European Jews came through the port of Hamburg on their journey to the United States, and you may locate your ancestors on these lists. The lists contain the name of the town of origin. They are available on microfilm through the LDS (Mormon) Family History Library. The FHL has a Source Guide to using Hamburg Emigration Lists (see section on "LDS [Mormon] Family History Library.")

Other Sources

Beyond these major sources described above, there are a host of other documents that might contain the name of the ancestral town.

• *Census records.* Rarely do census records have more than country of birth, but some people have reported that the census taker sometimes accidentally included town or region. For the 1920 census, the instructions to the census takers stated they were to list the province of birth for those born in the former Russian and Austrian Empire. The instructions were not always followed.

• *Vital records (birth, marriage, and death certificates).* These often list place of birth, but invariably, for an immigrant, only country is shown. Again, included might be town or region.

• *Burial societies.* Jewish immigrants formed *landsmanshaftn* societies that were social and help groups organized around a town of origin. The groups had burial committees that bought land in Jewish cemeteries and then sold plots to its members. If your ancestor was buried in a *landsmanshaftn* society plot, it may indicate that was his/her town of birth.

• *Social Security applications.* When a person applied for the Social Security program, starting in 1937, a question on the application was place of birth; therefore, town of birth may be shown.

• World War I Draft Registration Cards, 1917–18. For men born between 1886 and 1897 (whether citizens or aliens), this documentation gives the exact place of birth: city/town, state/province, country.

• *Obituary notices.* Items published in local secular and Jewish newspapers often contain more accurate details than official death certificates.

• *Probate records.* Wills and administrations can contain clues. Filed on the county level. Addresses of all U.S. county courthouses can be found in *Ancestry's Red Book* or *County Courthouse Book* (Genealogical Pub. Co., 2nd ed., 1995).

• *Alien registration*. Required of all non-citizens after 1941. Write to Immigration & Naturalization Service, Freedom of Information Office, Room 5304, 425 Eye Street NW, Washington, DC 20536 (202) 514-1554.

• *Surname clues*. If your surname is very unusual, consult Alexander Beider's *A Dictionary of Jewish Surnames from the Russian Empire* or *A Dictionary of Jewish Surnames from the Kingdom of Poland*. Some surnames are found only in a particular locality in Eastern Europe and these books will tell you in which district the author found your surname.

TREASURY DEPARTMENT
INTERNAL REVENUE SERVICE
U. S. SOCIAL SECURITY ACT
APPLICATION FOR ACCOUNT NUMBER 135-09-9122

1. SOLOMON BENJAMIN AUERBACH 612
2. 2535 Cruger ave. Bronx New York
4. Kleinman Br. 5. 366 5 7 A New York
6. 38 7. Oct. 3 1898 8. Kishineff Bess.
9. Benjamin J. Auerbach 10. Brana J. Gurtenste

11. SEX: MALE ✓ FEMALE 12. COLOR: WHITE ✓ NEGRO OTHER

13. IF REGISTERED WITH THE U. S. EMPLOYMENT SERVICE, GIVE NUMBER OF REGISTRATION CARD

14. IF YOU HAVE PREVIOUSLY FILLED OUT A CARD LIKE THIS, STATE

Nov. 28, 1936 16. Salomon Auerbach

DETACH ALONG THIS LINE

Social Security Application*: This application to participate in the Social Security program, filled out in 1936 by an immigrant, shows his parents' names (including mother's maiden name) and applicant's date and place of birth (Kishineff, Russia—today, Chisinau, Moldova).*

Special Problem: My Name Was Changed at Ellis Island

One of the great myths of immigration to the United States is that immigrants, especially Jewish immigrants, had their names changed at Ellis Island. According to Marian Smith, Historian for the Immigration and Naturalization Service, there is no evidence that this ever occurred. What did happen, in the majority of cases, is that Jewish immigrants, shortly after landing in the United States, discarded their European surnames and Americanized them due to social pressure "to become an American." Names were also changed because of anti-immigrant, anti-Semitic attitudes of Americans.

The scene of immigrants standing in line at Ellis Island shouting out their names to a non-Yiddish speaking clerk is a myth. Jews, as well as other immigrants, came with documentation of who they were. Their names were recorded on the ship's manifest for the very purpose of permitting U.S. immigration officials to check off the aliens as they passed through Ellis Island. The immigrant's name was accurately written on these manifests. In fact, one of the best sources for an accurate spelling of a European surname as well as the town of ancestry is the ship's manifest.

What do you do if your family's name was changed and no one in the family remembers the real name?

Name Changes in the United States

If the name was changed in the U.S., there are two major sources: naturalization and passenger arrival records.

If the immigrant became a citizen, check his Petition for Naturalization or accompanying Certificate of Arrival. It may show the original name.

A passenger arrival record approach is more circuitous. If the naturalization record does not have the original name, it will show the name of the ship on which the immigrant arrived and the date of arrival. Check *Morton Allan Directory of European Passenger Steamship Arrivals* to confirm that the ship arrived on that date. If it is within a day or two of the date the immigrant claimed, assume it is correct. Go to the ship's manifest. You know that somewhere on the many pages is the entry for your ancestor with his European name. There is a column on the manifest called "Race or Nationality." You can eliminate all persons not identified as "Hebrew," which is the way Jews were identified. You likely know the approximate age of your ancestor and his Yiddish name. Let us assume his first name was Izzie in the U.S., but his tombstone shows his name was Yitzhak. His naturalization papers (or family legend) state he arrived when he was 19 years old. You now can scan the ship's manifest for a person whose race is Hebrew, about 19 years old, whose first name was any of the European spellings of Yitzhak, including Isaac, Icek, Izik, etc. Once you find a possible hit, read the rest of the entry. Does the place of origin agree with family lore? Does the name of the person and place where he was going agree? From these facts, you will be able to locate your ancestor's entry and, consequently, his European surname.

Name Changes in Europe

If family legend states that the name was changed in Europe, you have a much more difficult task. Here is a possible strategy. You must determine your ancestral town. You must have access to the vital records of the town (or hire a professional researcher who has access). You must know some information about the family in Europe, such as the given names of family members. You must know the time frame of the family's residence in the town.

Example: Your great-grandfather, Morris Forlehrer, came to the United States, but family legend says Forlehrer was not his name in Europe; he changed it to avoid the onerous draft laws of the Russian Empire. It would appear that is all you know, but there is more you can gather. Using the suggestions in the chapter on "Finding Your Ancestral Town" you determine he was born in Radom, Poland. Go to his gravesite and read the tombstone inscription. It says he was "Moshe ben Yitzhak; died 1935, at age 62."

Armed with this information, you can now look at the birth records of Radom for a male child born about 1873; birth name, in Polish, likely Mosziek; father's name, likely Icek. If you find one or more records that fit this profile, the birth record will provide the mother's name. Look in other years for other children born to the couple. Jews name their children after deceased relatives. Knowing now the given names of this family unit, do they coincide with the religious names of members of your family?

Documenting Your Research Using Computers

If you know how to use a PC, as early in your research as possible, start maintaining your family history using one of the many genealogical software programs available at computer stores. If you maintain the data on paper, sooner or later—more likely sooner than later—you will be keying all the paper information into a computer.

Computerizing your information will make it easier to update. If the original information was incorrect, you do not need an eraser to correct the data, you just overtype the incorrect information. As your family tree grows into hundreds of people, finding a specific person can be difficult using paper documents. Genealogical software has a host of search features that allow you to locate an individual. By far, the most valuable advantage of computerizing is the many reports that can be produced with genealogical software [see examples on pages 39 and 66]. You can produce trees, narrative reports, exception reports, reasonability checks, and other functions.

Which Genealogy Software to Use

There are many computer software programs available to help you organize your family records, print charts and trees, etc. Many include capabilities that can be easily adapted for use by Jewish genealogists by adding custom fields such as Hebrew name, namesake (person named after), *yahrzeit* date, immigration date, etc.

There are books and a magazine, *Genealogical Computing*, that can advise you which package to purchase, but anything published is likely to be out-of-date as soon as it is in print, because the field is highly competitive and, therefore, ever improving. When selecting a software package, consult other genealogists to determine what they are using. They may even be willing to give you a demonstration.

There are dozens of programs on the market. Whichever you choose, be sure that the program includes GEDCOM capability. GEDCOM is a file format that allows information to be exchanged between programs. If you decide you do not like the software you are using, you can buy a different package, export your data in GEDCOM format from the old system, and import it into the new system. GEDCOM will also allow you to share portions of your database with other genealogists. You need GEDCOM in order to submit your data to the Family Tree of the Jewish

People (discussed elsewhere in this book).

Our opinions of the popular packages are:

• *Family Tree Maker.* Versions for DOS, Windows, PowerMac. Broderbund, P.O. Box 6125, Novato, CA 94948-6125 (800); 548-1804. Available at most software stores. Very easy to use. Highly recommended for beginners. Web: <http://www.familytreemaker.com>.

• *Reunion* (for Macintosh). Version 6.01. Leister Productions, P.O. Box 289, Mechanicsburg, PA 17055; (717) 697-1378. E-mail: <info@LeisterPro.com>. Web: <http://www.leisterpro.com>. Best genealogy program for the Macintosh. Very powerful program with graphical user interfaces. Good chart-making capabilities. (The Windows version is sold by Sierra, Inc. under the name Generations.)

• *Generations.* (Formerly "Reunion for Windows"). Version 6.0: "Generations Grande Suite." $50. Sierra, Inc.; (800) 757-7707. Web: <http://www.sierra.com/titles/generations>.

• *The Master Genealogist.* Version 4.0 for Windows. Wholly Genes Software, Inc., 5144 Flowertuft Court, Columbia, MD 21044; (800) 982-2103. E-mail: <76366.1760@CompuServe.com>. Web: <http://www.whollygenes.com>.

• *Brother's Keeper*, version 5.2F. For DOS and Windows. Shareware. John Steed, 6907 Chilsdale Rd., Rockford, MI 49341; (616) 364-5503. E-mail: <74774.650@compuserve.com>. The best of the shareware programs. Available for downloading from the Internet: <http://www.brokeep.com>.

• *Personal Ancestral File.* Version 4.0 for Windows. Freeware. Version 3.0 for DOS ($15); Version 2.31 for Macintosh ($35). Salt Lake Distribution Center, 1999 West 1700 South, Salt Lake City, UT 84104-4233; (801) 240-2584. The official software of the Mormon Church.

Cite Your Sources

This is the most underutilized aspect of genealogy. People acquire information and fail to document their sources. Documenting keeps you from forgetting. Very rapidly you become involved in situations where you will have conflicting information.

Example: You used the Social Security Death Index (SSDI) to get the birth and death dates of deceased members of your family and are entering the information into your database. You come to a person who already has a death date. It says February 1, 1972. The SSDI says February 1, 1973. Which one is correct? You don't know because you forgot the source of the entry already in the database. If it was a death certificate, you know the original entry is right and the SSDI is wrong (unless you keyed in the original information incorrectly). If the source of the original entry was an interview with a family member, you will want to call that person to resolve the discrepancy. Because you did not record the source of the original entry, you must go back to your file to determine its source—a time-consuming task.

All genealogical software programs have provisions for citing sources. Use the feature. If you want help in how to cite sources, read *Evidence! Citation & Analysis for the Family Historian* (see Appendix A).

1. **Menachem (Menkho) Tartasky** b. Abt 1810. That Yechaskel Tartasky's father was named Menachem is based on the 1912 Voter Registration list for Bialystok which identifies a Khatskel son of Menkho and the fact that Khatskel had a son named Mendel. This was confirmed on the birth record of Yeckaskel's son Shlomo.

1.1. **Yechazkel Tartasky** b. Abt 1830, m. (1) Taube ?, (daughter of Jossel ?) d. Bef 1910. Yechazkel died Abt 1910, Jerusalem, Palestine. After the death of his first wife, he married two more times. It is believed there were no children by these marriages. Taube: She predeceased her husband.

1.1.1. **Chaim Binyes Tartasky** (son of Yechazkel Tartasky and Taube ?) m. (1) Wife1 ?, m. (2) Ida ?. Chaim died Abt 1940. Ida: Yiddish name Chaia.

1.1.2. **Meir Tartasky** (son of Yechazkel Tartasky and Taube ?) b. Abt 1870, m. Rebecca Kagan. Meir died 1 Apr 1899. Rebecca: The arrival record of her son Sol refers to her given name as Bubke. A Bobke Taratatzki arrived in New York on 1 Jun 1909 listing her father in Poland as Yone (surname not legible). Going to brother-in-law, Solomon Grosstein.

1.1.3. **Zelig Tartasky** (son of Yechazkel Tartasky and Taube ?) m. Chaia ?.

1.1.4. **Joseph (Yankel/Yossel) Tatarsky** (son of Yechazkel Tartasky and Taube ?) m. Shifra Mines. Died 28 according to Chaia Tartasky Goldstein. He was in the bulding trades and fell off a ladder.

1.1.5. **Menachem Tartasky** (son of Yechazkel Tartasky and Taube ?) m. Stera ?. His given name is shown as Leib on the birth records of his sons Jacob and Joseph.

1.1.6. **Fruma Tartasky** (daughter of Yechazkel Tartasky and Taube ?).

1.1.7. **Aron Tartasky** (son of Yechazkel Tartasky and Taube ?) b. 25 Oct 1870, Bialystok, Poland. This person must have died young as he is not know to living members of the family.

1.1.8. **Shlomo Tartasky** (son of Yechazkel Tartasky and Taube ?) b. 6 Feb

Descendancy Report. *Most genealogical software programs provide a variety of reports based on the information you provide about each individual. This report shows the first three generations of the descendants of Menachem Tartasky.*

Glossary

Every discipline has its own jargon and abbreviations; Jewish genealogy is no exception. Below is a list of terms commonly used in Jewish genealogical research. Definitions of additional Yiddish and Hebrew words are at <http://www.jewishgen.org/infofiles/dict.txt>.

Ashkenazic [Heb] Of Jews whose origins are in Central and Eastern Europe.
brit, bris, brit milah [Heb] Circumcision ceremony that occurs seven days after the birth of a male child. It is at this ceremony that the boy receives his given name(s).
chevra kadisha [Heb] Burial society. Jews have created these social/religious groups to assure people are given a proper Jewish burial. They buy land or plots in a Jewish cemetery and offer members grave sites.
guberniya [Rus] Province of the czarist Russian Empire, pre-1917. There were 15 guberniyas in the Pale of Settlement and 10 guberniyas in the Polish provinces (Kingdom of Poland).
kehilla (pl. **kehillot**) [Heb] Jewish community. At times in the history of Eastern Europe, the kehilla was a legal entity with powers given by the governing country, such as the power to resolve disputes.
ketuba (pl. **ketubot**) [Heb] Jewish marriage contract, usually written in Aramaic.
landsman (pl. **landslayt**) [Yid] Townsman, someone from the same town.
landsmanshaft (pl. **landsmanshaftn**) [Yid] Township society; organization of people from the same ancestral town/village.
mishpacha [Heb/Yid] Family.
Pale of Settlement The only area of czarist Russia where Jews were permitted to live, although this rule was relaxed starting in the late 19th century. It consisted primarily of the areas Russia acquired when Poland was removed from the map in what were known as the three partitions of Poland that occurred in 1772, 1793, and 1795.
Sephardic [Heb] Of Jews whose origins are in medieval Spain.
shtetl (pl. **shtetlach**) [Yid] Small town, village. As used in genealogy, it has come to mean town of ancestry independent of the size of the town.
yichus [Heb] Pedigree; family background. [Yid] family status; prestige.
yizkor [Heb] Memorial, remembrance. Usually used in association with a series of books called yizkor books that memorialize towns where Jews lived before the Holocaust.

Abbreviations

AJHS	American Jewish Historical Society. An institution located in New York City that has an archives and library focusing on the Jewish presence in the Americas.
FHC	Family History Center, a branch of the LDS Family History Library. There are more than 2,000 centers located throughout the world.
FHL	Family History Library of the LDS (Mormon) Church located in Salt Lake City, Utah. It is the largest genealogy library in the world.
FHLC	Family History Library Catalog. The catalog that shows the holdings of the LDS Family History Library. It is available online, in microfiche form, and at all Family History Centers (FHC).
FTJP	Family Tree of the Jewish People. A database of family trees submitted by Jewish genealogists throughout the world.
HIAS	Hebrew Immigrant Aid Society. A social service organization that helps Jewish immigrants relocate in the United States.
IAJGS	International Association of Jewish Genealogical Societies. The umbrella group of Jewish Genealogical Societies.
INS	U.S. Immigration and Naturalization Service. The department of the U.S. government responsible for immigration and naturalization matters.
JGFF	JewishGen Family Finder. A database of ancestral surnames and towns being researched by more than 30,000 genealogists throughout the world.
JGS	Jewish Genealogical Society. An organization of genealogists who live in a given geographic area. Some members have interests in the geographic area.
LDS	Church of Jesus Christ of the Latter-day Saints. The Mormon Church. Their Family History Library (FHL) has the largest collection of genealogical records in the world. It includes Jewish records.
LOC	Library of Congress. The library of the United States government located in Washington, D.C.
NARA	National Archives and Records Administration. The archives of the United States government.

SIG	Special Interest Group. An group of genealogists organized by geographic area of ancestry or some other special interest.
SSDI	Social Security Death Index. A database of more than 60 million people who died in the U.S. since 1960 for whom there was a Social Security death claim. It likely represents more than 90% of Americans who died since 1960.
USHMM	United States Holocaust Memorial Museum. A U.S. government institution located in Washington, D.C. Included are an archives and library that contain material regarding the Holocaust.
WOWW	*Where Once We Walked*, a gazetteer of some 22,000 towns in Central and Eastern Europe where Jews lived before the Holocaust.

Appendix A: Useful Books for Jewish Genealogical Research

There are numerous books available to assist you in your research. One publisher, Avotaynu, Inc., focuses specifically on books for Jewish genealogy. It has published some 20 books on the subject during the past eight years. Below are some titles and other information about books oriented toward the needs of Jewish genealogical research. Many are available in local libraries. If your library does not have a specific book, ask them if they can get it on interlibrary loan. Most of the books are in print and can be purchased if you wish to develop a genealogy library.

Avotaynu, Inc., has developed a list of "Recommended Books for a Jewish Genealogy Library." It ranks many of the books noted below from those mandatory, in its opinion, for such a library, to those less significant. This list can be found at <http://www.avotaynu.com/recommend.htm>.

American Genealogy

The Source: Revised Edition, edited by Loretto Dennis Szucs and Sandra Hargreaves Luebking (Salt Lake City: Ancestry, 1997). Considered by many to be the most comprehensive source of information about resources for American genealogy.

The Researcher's Guide to American Genealogy, by Val D. Greenwood (Baltimore: Genealogical Publishing Company, 1990). Another guide to American genealogy. It is the text of choice in colleges and universities and has been adopted by the National Genealogical Society as its basic text in home study courses. It is both a text book and an all-purpose reference book.

International Vital Records Handbook (New Third Edition), by Thomas J. Kemp (Baltimore: Genealogical Publishing Company, 1994). Forms for getting birth, marriage, and death records from every state and some countries.

State Census Records, by Ann S. Lainhart (Baltimore: Genealogical Publishing Company, 1990). Describes every state census taken in the U.S. and where to get the records.

Genealogist's Address Book (Fourth Edition), by Elizabeth Petty Bentley (Baltimore: Genealogical Publishing Company, 1999). Provides thousands of names, addresses, phone numbers, contact persons, and business hours of government agencies, societies, libraries, archives, professional bodies, periodicals, newspaper columns, publishers, booksellers, services, databases, bulletin boards, and more.

American Cities

Chicago and Cook County: A Guide to Research, by Loretto Dennis Szucs (Salt Lake City: Ancestry, 1996). A comprehensive guide to the vastly complex records of this major urban area that has been home to so many Jews and other immigrant groups. The book covers virtually every genealogical source, from architectural history to vital records.

Genealogical Resources in the New York Metropolitan Area, edited by Estelle M. Guzik (New York: Jewish Genealogical Society, Inc., 1989). Definitive work on genealogical resources in this important city of Jewish immigration. More than 100 facilities identified.

Resources for Jewish Genealogy in the Boston Area, by Warren Blatt (Boston: Jewish Genealogical Society of Greater Boston, 1996). Describes 22 sites in the Boston area that have information relevant to Jewish genealogical research.

American Immigration

They Came In Ships: A Guide to Finding Your Immigrant Ancestor's Arrival Record, by John P. Colletta. (Salt Lake City: Ancestry, 1993.) This book helps to navigate the researcher through the various indexes to passenger arrival records, books, and articles about the immigrant experience. The author discusses what you need to know to begin your search and suggests the most likely places to find that information.

They Became Americans: Finding Naturalization Records and Ethnic Origins, by Loretto Dennis Szucs (Salt Lake City: Ancestry, Inc., 1998). Naturalization (citizenship) records rank as one of the important sources of information in Jewish genealogy. Often, they are difficult to find, and their information can be confusing. This book is a generously illustrated guide to it all.

Guide to Naturalization Records of the United States, by Christina Schaefer (Baltimore: Genealogical Publishing Co., 1997). State by state, county by county, city by city, this book identifies all repositories of naturalization records, systematically indicating the types of records held (declarations of intention, petitions for naturalization, case files, indexes, etc.), dates of coverage, and location of original and microfilm records.

American Naturalization Records 1790–1990: What They Are and How to Use Them, by John J. Newman (Bountiful, UT: Heritage Quest, 1998).

Migration from the Russian Empire—Vol. 1–6 (Baltimore: Genealogical Publishing Company, 1995+). Index to passengers arriving in the

United States from the Russian Empire from 1875–91. The passenger arrival records for this time period were never indexed by the U.S. government.

Morton Allan Directory of European Passenger Steamship Arrivals (Baltimore: Genealogical Publishing Company, reprinted 1987). Lists steamship arrivals for the years 1890–1930 for the Port of New York and 1904–1926 for New York and Philadelphia, Boston, and Baltimore. Jewish genealogists find this a useful reference to verify arrival dates noted on family documents, determine arrival dates of ancestors when only the ship name is known, or determine ship name when only the arrival date is known.

American Passenger Arrival Records, by Michael Tepper (Baltimore: Genealogical Publishing Co., 1988, 1993). Scholarly, comprehensive guide.

Immigrant and Passenger Arrivals: A Select Catalog of National Archives Microfilm Publications (Washington: National Archives Trust Fund Board, 1983, 1991). Reel-by-reel listing of all microfilms of passenger lists.

American Jewish

Encyclopedia of Jewish Genealogy, Volume 1—Sources in the U.S. and Canada, by Arthur Kurzweil and Miriam Weiner (Northvale, N.J.: Jason Aronson, 1991). Describes the vast amount of Jewish-oriented material available to the researcher in the United States and Canada and how to access it. Specific sections focus on resources in states with large Jewish populations and detail the exceptionally useful documents at the LDS (Mormon) Family History Library.

Beginners Guides

From Generation to Generation, by Arthur Kurzweil (New York: HarperCollins, 1994). A popular beginner's guide to Jewish genealogy. This pioneer work, originally published in 1980, has been revised and updated. It is both inspirational and informative.

Documents of Our Ancestors: A Selection of Reproducible Genealogy Forms and Tips for Using Them, by Michael J. Meshenberg (Teaneck N.J.: Avotaynu, 1995). Includes dozens of search and record forms of U.S. government census records, passenger records, World War I draft registrations, naturalization petitions and declarations of intention, alien registrations, requests for veteran's records and Social Security forms, and more.

Do People Grow on Family Trees: Genealogy for Kids & Other

Beginners, by Ira Wolfman (New York: Workmens Publishing Company, 1991). This delightfully written book is crammed full of photos, cartoons, and charts to explain the basis of genealogical research. Immigration, naturalization, Ellis Island, surnames, and much more are presented.

Finding Our Fathers, by Dan Rottenberg. (Reprinted by Baltimore: Genealogical Publishing Company, 1995.) Pioneer beginner's guide to Jewish genealogy. Obsolete, but still some useful suggestions. Published in 1977, this was the first book on Jewish genealogical research. It has not been updated since.

Compiled Genealogies

Compiled genealogies are published family trees, usually the descendants of some famous person.

Sourcebook for Jewish Genealogies and Family Histories, by David Zubatsky and Irwin Berent (Teaneck, N.J.: Avotaynu, 1996). Sources for information about 11,000 Jewish family names. The most comprehensive bibliography for published and unpublished Jewish genealogies, family histories, and individual family names.

The Unbroken Chain, by Neil Rosenstein (Elizabeth, N.J.: Computer Center for Jewish Genealogy, 1990). 25,000 descendants of the founder of the Katzenellenbogen family. A pioneer work in Jewish compiled genealogies.

Eliyahu's Branches: The Descendants of the Vilna Gaon and His Family, by Chaim Freedman (Teaneck, N.J.: Avotaynu, 1998). This book documents some 20,000 descendants of this great rabbi and scholar.

The Gaon of Vilna and his Cousinhood, by Neil Rosenstein (Elizabeth, N.J.: Computer Center for Jewish Genealogy, 1997). Charts of descendants of the Vilna Gaon and related families. Does not contain the detail of the Freedman work.

The Book of Destiny: Toledot Charlap, by Arthur F. Menton (Cold Spring Harbor, N.Y.: King David Press, 1996). The Charlaps are traced from Eastern Europe back to Spain and Portugal, and from the Babylonian exile to the royal families of Judah and Israel.

Ancilla to Toledot Charlap, by Arthur Menton (Cold Spring Harbor, N.Y.: King David Press, 1999). Meant as a companion piece to *Book of Destiny: Toledot Charlap* or can be used on its own. This book gives detailed information as well as 337 charts and family trees on this distinguished Charlap family.

Scattered Seeds, by George Sackheim (Self-published, 1986). Descendants of Rabbi Israel; the Zak family.

First American Jewish Families (Third Edition), by Rabbi Malcolm H.

Stern (Baltimore: Ottenheimer Publishers, 1991) The definitive work on the Jewish families that arrived during the Colonial/Federal period (1654–1838).

Europe—General

In Search of Your European Roots, by Angus Baxter (Baltimore: Genealogical Publishing Company, 1985). A shallow overview of record searching in Europe. Guidebook for doing genealogy in 44 European countries crammed into 292 pages. Little Jewish information.

General Jewish

Avotaynu on CD-ROM—all back issues (1985–1999) (Teaneck, N.J.: Avotaynu, 2000). The most comprehensive reference work on Jewish genealogy. More than 1,500 articles, 2,300 pages, 2 million words; all accessible using a search engine.

Holocaust

How to Document Victims and Locate Survivors of the Holocaust, by Gary Mokotoff (Teaneck, N.J.: Avotaynu, 1995). How-to book of Holocaust research. It identifies the principal sources of information about Holocaust victims and survivors, identifies the major repositories in the world that have this information, and tells how to contact them. It takes you step-by-step through the process for locating information about the fate of people caught up in the Holocaust.

German Minority Census of 1939: Introduction and Register, by Thomas Kent Edlund (Teaneck, N.J.: Avotaynu, 1998). Identifies the microfilm numbers for each of the German towns in the LDS (Mormon) Family History Library microfilm collection of this important Holocaust-era census. Information in the actual census records includes name, birth date, place of birth, which of the person's four grandparents were Jewish.

Vilniaus Getas (Vilnius Ghetto): Lists of Prisoners, by Jewish State Museum of Lithuania (Vilnius: Jewish State Museum of Lithuania, 1998). This two-volume work contains 15,300 names of Jews living in the Vilnius Ghetto in 1942, listed by street address, together with interesting articles and information written in English. Volume 2 lists the names and information about the Jews living in the various work camps in the vicinity of Vilnius.

How-To Books on Genealogy

Evidence! Citation & Analysis for the Family Historian (Baltimore: Genealogical Publishing Company, 1997), by Elizabeth Shown Mills. No family history is complete without proper source citations and sound analysis of evidence. This book provides the guidelines and explicit models for proper genealogical documentation.

How to Tape Instant Oral Biographies, by Bill Zimmerman (Cincinnati: Betterway Books, 1999). This book tells how to interview people and use a tape or video recorder to create a living record. It suggests questions to ask and describes how to use pictures and documents.

Organizing Your Family History Search, by Sharon DeBartolo Carmack, CG (Cincinnati: Betterway Books, 1999). A book filled with ideas, solutions, and forms to assist you in properly organizing and performing your research. It covers areas such as creating filing systems, handling correspondence, planning research trips, and others.

Producing a Quality Family History, by Patricia Law Hatcher, CG (Salt Lake City: Ancestry, 1996). This book focuses on the steps and considerations required in the process of assembling and printing a family history book.

To Our Children's Children: Preserving Family Histories for Generations to Come, by Bob Greene and D. G. Fulford (New York: Doubleday, 1993). Contains a list of more than 1,000 questions you should consider asking when interviewing people; starting with "What is your name?" to "If you hold a fundamental truth, what is it?"

Internet

Netting Your Ancestors, by Cyndi Howells (Baltimore: Genealogical Publishing Company, 1999). A primer on how to use the Internet for genealogical research. There are chapters on e-mail, mailing lists, and the World Wide Web explaining what they are and strategies for how to use them.

Israel

A Guide to Jewish Genealogical Resources in Israel, by Sallyann Amdur Sack and the Israel Genealogical Society (Teaneck, N.J.: Avotaynu, 1995). The definitive work on the resources for Jewish genealogy located in the libraries and archives of Israel. It contains information about more than 25 repositories in Israel with in-depth descriptions of their holdings and how to reach them by mail or phone.

Names

A Dictionary of Jewish Surnames from the Russian Empire, by Alexander Beider (Teaneck, N.J.: Avotaynu, 1993). This landmark work is a compilation of 50,000 Jewish surnames from the Russian Pale of Settlement (excluding the Kingdom of Poland). Shows etymology, name variants, and where within the Russian Empire the name appeared. An introductory section describes the origins and evolution of Jewish surnames from this region.

A Dictionary of Jewish Surnames from the Kingdom of Poland, by Alexander Beider. (Teaneck, N.J.: Avotaynu, 1996.) More than 33,000 Jewish surnames found in that part of the Russian Empire known as the "Kingdom of Poland." Comparable in structure to its predecessor book: *A Dictionary of Jewish Surnames from the Russian Empire*.

Ancient Ashkenazic Surnames: Jewish Surnames from Prague (15th–18th Centuries), by Alexander Beider (Teaneck, N.J.: Avotaynu, 1995). Origins of some of the earliest Ashkenazic surnames. This short work identifies 700 surnames from the ancient city of Prague from the 15th to 18th centuries.

Complete Dictionary of English and Hebrew First Names, by Alfred J. Kolatch (Middle Village, N. Y.: Jonathan David, 1984). Included among the more than 11,000 main entries are a large number of Biblical names plus practically every Hebrew first name used in Israel today.

Russian-Jewish Given Names: Their Origins and Variants, by Boris Feldblyum (Teaneck, N.J.: Avotaynu, 1998). A comprehensive collection of Jewish given names used in Russia at the turn of the 20th century—more than 6,000 names in all. These names are also included in a dictionary of root names that shows the etymology as well as all variants identifying them as kinnui (everyday names), variants, or distortions.

A Dictionary of Jewish Names and Their History, by Benzion C. Kaganoff (Northvale: N.J.: Jason Aronson, 1996). Pioneer work on this subject, it has been surpassed by the works of Alexander Beider.

Places

Where Once We Walked, by Gary Mokotoff and Sallyann Amdur Sack (Teaneck, N.J.: Avotaynu, 1991). Landmark gazetteer of 22,000 towns in Central and Eastern Europe where Jews lived before the Holocaust. Includes 15,000 alternate names allowing readers to locate town by previous names and Yiddish names. Gives latitude/longitude, Jewish population before the Holocaust, and cites as many as 40 books that reference each town.

WOWW Companion, by Gary Mokotoff (Teaneck, N.J.: Avotaynu, 1995). This book lists, in sequence by latitude/longitude, the 22,000 towns identified in *Where Once We Walked*, making it easy to isolate towns that are close to a specific town. Finding places located 10, 20, 30, or more miles from a given town is possible using this book.

Shtetl Finder, by Chester Cohen (Bowie, Maryland: Heritage Books,

1980). A favorite among Jewish genealogists, this book lists some 1,200 towns in Central and Eastern Europe identifying famous persons from the town and/or pre-publication subscribers to turn-of-the-century books.

Resources by Country

Alsace. *Index to the 1784 Census of the Jews of Alsace*. (Teaneck, N.J.: Avotaynu, 1995). Microfiche that documents some 20,000 Jews who were enumerated in this census.

Canada. *Jewish Residents of Canada in the 1861–1901 Censuses of Canada*. (Teaneck, N.J.: Avotaynu, 1995.) Microfiche list of all Jews found in five Canadian censuses.

Canada. *A Biographical Dictionary of Canadian Jewry—1909–1914*, by Lawrence F. Tapper. (Teaneck, N.J.: Avotaynu, 1995.) Births, bar mitzvahs, marriages, and deaths, as well as information concerning communal and synagogue activities of Canadian Jewry. Taken from the pages of *The Canadian Jewish Times*.

France/Holocaust. *Index to Memorial to the Jews Deported from France*. (Teaneck, N.J.: Avotaynu, 1993.) Alphabetical list on microfiche of 50,000 surnames that appear in *Memorial to Jews Deported From France*. Shows surname and convoy number.

Galicia. *Finding Your Jewish Roots in Galicia: A Resource Guide*, by Suzan F. Wynne (Teaneck, N.J.: Avotaynu, 1998). Definitive work on researching your Galician roots. This book organizes what is known about Galician-Jewish record searching and other resources to assist genealogists in tracing their Jewish-Galician roots. Such resources include archival collections of Jewish vital and other records; geographic, visual and language aides; books; and documents related to the Holocaust. The book directs you to addresses of archives, researchers, and translators, as well as organizations that hold important resource information.

Germany. *Germanic Genealogy: A Guide to Worldwide Sources & Migrations* (St. Paul, Minnesota: Germanic Genealogy Society, 1991). A country-by-country guide to sources giving addresses of repositories. There is a chapter devoted specifically to German-Jewish genealogical resources. The best book for persons with German-Jewish ancestry.

Library Resources for German-Jewish Genealogy, by Angelika G. Ellmann-Krüger with Edward David Luft (Teaneck, N.J.: Avotaynu, 1998). A concise directory of library sources that are valuable additions to archival resources and how these sources can be used efficiently. It describes information found in monographs, periodical articles, or collective works, such as family histories, genealogies, autobiographies, and biographies.

Hungary. (Teaneck, N.J.: Avotaynu, 1998). There are a number of microfiche collections. *Birth Index for Buda Jewry, 1820–1852, 1868.* Index to certain Jewish birth records of Budapest. *Obuda Census of 1850: Index and Complete Census. Mako and Battonya (Hungary) Vital and Census Records, 1824–1880.*

Israel. *A Guide to Jewish Genealogical Resources in Israel*, by Sallyann Amdur Sack and the Israel Genealogical Society. (Teaneck, N.J.: Avotaynu, 1996). Resources for Jewish genealogy located in the libraries and archives of Israel. This book contains information about more than 25 repositories in Israel with in-depth descriptions of their holdings and information on how to reach these repositories by mail or phone.

Lithuania. *Jewish Vital Records, Revision Lists and Other Jewish Holdings in the Lithuanian Archives*, by Harold Rhode and Sallyann Amdur Sack (Teaneck, N.J.: Avotaynu, 1998). An index to Jewish vital records in the Lithuanian archives, some as early as 1808, and revision lists (censuses), some as early as 1795. There are 12,000 entries for more than 220 towns.

Moldova. *Jewish Roots in Ukraine and Moldova: Pages from the Past and Archival Inventories*, by Miriam Weiner (Secaucus, N.J.: Miriam Weiner Routes to Roots Foundation, 1999). Archival inventories representing 1,400 shtetls and towns prepared with the help of the archives of Ukraine and Moldova.

Morocco. *Noms des Juifs du Maroc—Moroccan Jewish Surnames.* (Teaneck, N.J.: Avotaynu, 1994.) Microfiche index to the Laredo book on the subject.

Palestine. *Palestine Gazette.* (Teaneck, N.J.: Avotaynu, 1990.) Microfiche index of 28,000 people who legally changed their names in Palestine, 1921–48.

Poland. *Jewish Roots in Poland: Pages from the Past and Archival Inventories*, by Miriam Weiner (Secaucus, N.J.: Miriam Weiner Routes to Roots Foundation, 1997). The most complete inventory of surviving Jewish records in Poland. Filled with many color pictures of towns and Jewish life in Poland.

Romania. *Romanian Census Records.* (Teaneck, N.J.: Avotaynu, 1995). Microfiche of Romanian census of Jews taken in 1825. Index to the census of Jews in 1824–25. 1852 census of Jews of Monesti.

Russian Empire. *Index to Russian Consular Records.* (Teaneck, N.J.: Avotaynu, 1995) Microfiche of index to a collection at the U.S. National Archives. 70,000 people who did business with the czarist consulates in the U.S.

Slovakia. *Jewish Vital Statistics Records in Slovakian Archives* (Teaneck, N.J.: Avotaynu, 1995). Microfiche that shows what Jewish vital records exist in which archives in Slovakia. Shown are year, type of records (birth, marriage, death) and location of records.

Ukraine. *Jewish Roots in Ukraine and Moldova: Pages from the Past and Archival Inventories*, by Miriam Weiner (Secaucus, N.J.: Miriam Weiner Routes to Roots Foundation, 1999). Archival inventories representing 1,400 shtetls and towns prepared with the help of the archives of Ukraine and Moldova.

Translating Records

Following the Paper Trail: A Multilingual Translation Guide, by Jonathan D. Shea and William F. Hoffman (Teaneck, N.J.: Avotaynu, 1994). A guide to translating vital statistic records and other genealogy-related records in 13 languages: Czech, French, German, Hungarian, Italian, Latin, Lithuanian, Polish, Portuguese, Romanian, Russian, Spanish, and Swedish. Each section shows the alphabet of the language, sample records and their translation, and a list of words commonly encountered.

Russian Language Documents from Russian Poland, by Jonathan Shea. Detailed guide for translating handwritten Russian records of births, deaths, and marriages of Russian Poland. Out of print.

A Translation Guide to 19th-Century Polish-Language Civil-Registration Documents, by Judith Frazin (Chicago: Jewish Genealogical Society of Illinois, 1989). Detailed, illustrated guide to translating Polish-language birth, marriage, and death records. Out of print. A revised addition is planned for Summer 2000.

Appendix B

Illustrations

RZECZPOSPOLITA POLSKA

URZĄD STANU CYWILNEGO w Sosnowcu---------------

Województwo katowickie----------------------------

Odpis skrócony aktu urodzenia

1. Nazwisko Wajngarten---------------------------
2. Imię (imiona) Szyja---------------------------
3. Data urodzenia pietnastego lipca tysiac dziewiećset dziesiatego (15.7.1910) roku---
4. Miejsce urodzenia Sosnowiec---------------------
5. Imię i nazwisko rodowe (ojca) Moszek Wajngarten---------
6. Imię i nazwisko rodowe (matki) Frajda Ruchla Koniecpolska-

Poświadcza się zgodność powyższego odpisu z treścią aktu urodzenia Nr 167/27/12

Sosnowiec, data 1994.02.23

Miejsce na opłatę skarbową

URZĄD STANU CYWILNEGO W SOSNOWCU

m.p.

KIEROWNIK
Urzędu Stanu Cywilnego

mgr inż. Arkadiusz Trzuskowski

Birth Record: *Transcript of a Polish birth record obtained from the civil registration office of Sosnowiec, Poland. It is the record of the birth of Szyja (Joshua) Wajngarten, son of Moszek (Moses) Wajngarten and Frajda Ruchla (Frieda Rachel) Koniecpolska. Transcripts are not as valuable as original records because of the risk of transcription error; original records often have additional valuable information, such as age of parents and from where they came.*

Health Department of the City of New York.

RETURN OF A MARRIAGE.

1. *Full Name of* HUSBAND, John Rosenbecker
2. *Place of Residence,* Guttenberg, N. J.
3. *Age next Birthday,* 24 *years,*
4.
5. *Occupation,* brewer
6. *Place of Birth,* Steinfurt, Hassia-Darmstadt, Gy
7. *Father's Name,* Henry Rosenbecker
8. *Mother's Maiden Name,* Catharine Huber
9. *No. of Husband's Marriage,* first
10. *Full Name of* WIFE, Catharine Nufs

    Maiden Name, if a Widow,

11. *Place of Residence,* Guttenberg, N. J.
12. *Age next Birthday* 23 *years,*
13.
14. *Place of Birth,* Moerzheim, Landau, Bavaria
15. *Father's Name,* John Nufs
16. *Mother's Maiden Name,* Eva Marie Boebinger
17. *No. of Wife's Marriage,* first

N. B.—At Nos. 4 and 13 state if Colored; If other races, specify what. At Nos. 9 and 17 state whether 1st, 2d, 3d, &c., Marriage of each.

New York, June 9th 1872

We, the Husband and Wife named in the above Certificate, hereby Certify that the information given is correct, to the best of our knowledge and belief.

John Rosenbecker *(Husband.)*

Catharine Nufs *(Wife.)*

***Marriage Record**: This 1872 New York City marriage record includes the ages of the bride and groom; places of birth in Germany; and names of parents, including maiden names of mothers.*

[illegible] A. 35, die Beglaubigung von Todesfällen betreffend) ist der Leopold
Loewenherz, Sohn des [illegible] Kaufmann Abraham Loewenherz und Rosa
geborene Meyer [illegible] Moses Stern zu Beverungen, zur Religionsgesellschaft der Juden gehörend, geboren am ersten Februar achtzehnhundert
[illegible] und sechzig, am zwölften Februar achtzehnhundert fünf und sechzig
Nachmittags vier Uhr an der [illegible] gestorben. – Eingetragen Beverungen
am dreizehnten Februar achtzehnhundert fünf und sechzig.
[illegible] [illegible] [illegible] Protokollführer

88. Nach der Anzeige vom 22ten Februar 1865 (fol 136 der Spezial-Akten [illegible] Ge-
neral-Akten A. 35, die Beglaubigung von Todesfällen betreffend) ist die Adele
Kohlberg, Tochter des [illegible] Kaufmann Jacob Lehmann Kohlberg und
Hannchen geborene Rothschild zu Beverungen, zur Religionsgesellschaft
der Juden gehörend, geboren am zehnten März achtzehnhundert ein und sechzig,
am ein und zwanzigsten Februar achtzehnhundert fünf und sechzig Morgens acht
Uhr am Magenfieber gestorben. – Eingetragen Beverungen am zwei und
zwanzigsten Februar achtzehnhundert fünf und sechzig –
[illegible] [illegible] [illegible] Protokollführer

89. Nach der Anzeige vom 24ten July 1865 (fol 137 der Spezial-Akten [illegible] der Ge-
neral-Akten A. 35, die Beglaubigung von Todesfällen betreffend) ist der Louis Maas

***Death Record**: German death register. Document #88 records the death of Adele Kohlberg, daughter of Jacob Lehmann Kohlberg and Hannchen Rothchild of Beverungen. The deceased was born on March 10, 1861, and died on February 21, 1865.*

2343

U. S. DEPARTMENT OF LABOR
NATURALIZATION SERVICE

No.

DUPLICATE
(To be forwarded to the Bureau of Naturalization)

UNITED STATES OF AMERICA

68751

PETITION FOR NATURALIZATION

To the Honorable the Supreme Court of the State of New York, County of Bronx
The petition of Abraham Friedberg hereby filed, respectfully showeth:
First. My place of residence is 813 E 163 St (Give number and street) New York City, N. Y.
Second. My occupation is Bricklayer
Third. I was born on the 17 day of Sept anno Domini 1883, at Wilkovesk Russia
Fourth. I emigrated to the United States from Bremen Germany on or about the 15 day of Sept anno Domini 1904, and arrived in the United States, at the port of Baltimore Maryland on the 6 day of Oct anno Domini 1904 on the vessel Barbarossa
Fifth. I declared my intention to become a citizen of the United States on the 22 day of June anno Domini 1926 at NY in the US So District Court of NY
Sixth. I am married. My wife's name is Rose she was born on the 7 day of July anno Domini 1888 Russia and now resides at 813 E 163 St New York City, N. Y.
I have 9 children, and the name, date and place of birth, and place of residence of each of said children is as follows:
Hyman - 29 Sept 1906, Elaine - 2 Nov 1921, All born in NY City and reside
Peggy - 10 May 1908, Murray - 16 Sept 1923, with me
Sollie - 12 Apl 1910, Benjamin - 1 Aug 1925
Philip - 12 Jan 1912
Henry - 6 Feb 1914
Sylvia - 12 Jan 1918, Married Oct 25, 1907
Seventh. I am not a disbeliever in or opposed to organized government or a member of or affiliated with any organization or body of persons teaching disbelief in or opposed to organized government. I am not a polygamist nor a believer in the practice of polygamy. I am attached to the principles of the Constitution of the United States, and it is my intention to become a citizen of the United States and to renounce absolutely and forever all allegiance and fidelity to any foreign prince, potentate, state, or sovereignty, and particularly to The State of Russia - The Republic of Poland of whom at this time I am a subject, and it is my intention to reside permanently in the United States.
Eighth. I am able to speak the English language.
Ninth. I have resided continuously in the United States of America for the term of five years at least immediately preceding the date of this petition, to wit, since the 6 day of Oct, anno Domini 1904 and in the State of New York, continuously next preceding the date of this petition, since the 8 day of Oct, anno Domini 1904 being a residence within this State of at least one year next preceding the date of this petition.
Tenth. I have not heretofore made petition for citizenship to any court. (I made petition for citizenship to the ______ Court of ______ at ______ on the ______ day of ______, anno Domini ______, and the said petition was denied by the said Court for the following reasons and causes, to wit: ______ and the cause of such denial has since been cured or removed.)
Attached hereto and made a part of this petition are my declaration of intention to become a citizen of the United States and the certificate from the Department of Labor, together with my affidavit and the affidavits of the two verifying witnesses thereto, required by law. Wherefore your petitioner prays that he may be admitted a citizen of the United States of America.

Abraham Friedberg
(Complete and true signature of petitioner)

Declaration of Intention No. 193931 and Certificate of Arrival from Department of Labor filed this 20 day of Oct 1928

Note to Clerk of Court.—If petitioner arrived in the United States on or before June 29, 1906, strike out the words reading "and Certificate of Arrival from Department of Labor."

AFFIDAVITS OF PETITIONER AND WITNESSES

STATE OF NEW YORK, County of Bronx, ss:

The aforesaid petitioner being duly sworn, deposes and says that he is the petitioner in the above-entitled proceeding; that he has read the foregoing petition and knows the contents thereof; that the said petition is signed with his full, true name; that the same is true of his own knowledge, except as to matters therein stated to be alleged upon information and belief, and that as to those matters he believes it to be true.

Abraham Friedberg
(Complete and true signature of petitioner)

David Pollack occupation Bricklayer residing at 788 Brook [illegible] St
Isaie Siegel occupation Bricklayer residing at 753 [illegible] St
each being severally, duly, and respectively sworn, deposes and says that he is a citizen of the United States of America; that he has personally known Abraham Friedberg the petitioner above-mentioned, to have resided in the United States continuously

Petition for Naturalization: *The "Final Papers," filled out before being granted citizenship, contain a wealth of information about the applicant and family including the birth dates and places of the applicant, his wife, and children. It shows the applicant's marriage date, home address, occupation, date of arrival in the United States, and on what ship the applicant arrived.*

28

Required by the regulations of the Secretary of the Treasury of the United States, under Act o
Officer of any vessel having such passenger

S. S. Blücher sailing from Hamburg 8. Deze

1	2	3	4	5	6	7	8	9	10	
No. on List.	NAME IN FULL.	Age. Yrs. Mos.	Sex.	Married or Single.	Calling or Occupation.	Able to— Read. Write.	Nationality. (Country of last permanent residence.)	* Race or People.	Last Residence. (Province, City, or Town.)	Final De (St City, o

Passenger Arrival Record: A 1907 ship's manifest showing much information including age, race (Hebrew for Jews), last residence, and name and address where immigrant was going.

[illegible] Congress approved March 3, 1903, to be delivered to the U. S. Immigration Officer by the Commanding [illegible] on board upon arrival at a port in the United States.

[illegible]mber 1905, 190 *Arriving at Port of* New York Dec. 19, 190[illegible]

11	12	13	14	15	16	17	18	19	20	21
[illegible]stination. [illegible]ate, [illegible] Town.)	Whether having a ticket to such final destination.	By whom was passage paid?	Whether in possession of $50, and if less, how much?	Whether ever before in the United States; and if so, when and where?	Whether going to join a relative or friend; and if so, what relative or friend, and his name and complete address.	Ever in prison or almshouse, or institution for care and treatment of the insane, or supported by charity? If so, which?	Whether a Polygamist.	Whether an Anarchist.	[illegible]	Condition of Health, Mental and Physical.

9—167

DEPARTMENT OF COMMERCE—

FOURTEENTH CENSUS OF THE UNIT

STATE New York
COUNTY New York
TOWNSHIP OR OTHER DIVISION OF COUNTY Manhattan
NAME OF INCORPORA
NAME OF INSTITUTION x
ENU

Line	Street (1)	House number (2)	Dwelling no. (3)	Family no. (4)	Name (5)	Relation (6)	Home owned or rented (7)	Owned free or mortgaged (8)	Sex (9)	Color or race (10)	Age (11)	Single, married, widowed, or divorced (12)	Year of immigration (13)	Naturalized or alien (14)	Year of naturalization (15)	Attended school (16)	Able to read (17)	Able to write (18)	Place of birth (19)
51	East 118th Street	227	14	172	Katzman Sylvia	daughter			F	w	8	S				yes	yes	yes	New York
52					Dorothy	daughter			F	w	6	S				yes			New York
53				173	Bitterman Morris	Head 5	R		m	w	50	m	1912	al			no	no	Romania
54					Dora	wife			F	w	49	m	1912	al			no	no	Romania
55					Harry	son			m	w	24	S	1912	Na	1919		yes	yes	Romania
56					Joe	son			m	w	21	S	1912	al			yes	yes	Romania
57					Sam	son			m	w	19	S	1912	al			yes	yes	Romania
58					Jake	son			m	w	18	S	1912	al			yes	yes	Romania
59					Louie	son			m	w	16	S	1912	al			yes	yes	Romania
60					Jackobi Harry	Lodger			m	w	30	S	1915	al			no	no	Austria
61				174	Indlich Carl	Head 6	R		m	w	44	m	1912	Pa			yes	yes	Hungary
62		229	15	175	Platt Jacob B	Head 1	R		m	w	30	m	1894	Na	1912		yes	yes	Russia
63					Sadie	wife			F	w	21	m					yes	yes	New York
64					Leonard	son			m	w	1	S							New York
65				176	Eckstein Max	Head 2	R		m	w	36	m	1910	Pa			yes	yes	Austria
66					Tillie	wife			F	w	32	m	1910	Al			yes	yes	Austria
67					Louie	son			m	w	13	S	1910	Al		yes	yes	yes	Austria
68					Isaac	son			m	w	12	S	1910	Al		yes	yes	yes	Austria
69					Sadie	daughter			F	w	10	S	1910	Al		yes	yes	yes	Austria
70				177	Hiefhaber Edward	Head 3	R		m	w	42	m					yes	yes	New York
71					Lizzie	wife			F	w	35	m	1905	Na			yes	yes	Hungary
72					John	son			m	w	16	S				yes	yes	yes	New York
73					Charlie	son			m	w	12	S				yes	yes	yes	New York
74					Andrew	son			m	w	8	S				yes	yes	yes	New York
75					Esther	daughter			F	w	5	S				yes			New York
76				178	Seigel Sarah	Head 4	R		F	w	51	wd	1913	al			no	no	Romania
77					Bessy	daughter			F	w	24	S	1913	al			yes	yes	Romania
78					Morris	son			m	w	22	S	1913	al			yes	yes	Romania
79				179	Mohotoff Joe	Head 5	R		m	w	35	m	1906	Na	1916		yes	yes	Russia
80					Sele	wife			F	w	37	m	1906	Na	1916		yes	yes	Russia
81					Max	son			m	w	9	S				yes	yes	yes	New York
82					Lipshitz Mary	Lodger			F	w	23	S	1918	al			no	no	Russia
83				180	Rozenblatt Celia	Head 6	R		F	w	43	wd	1901	al			yes	yes	Austria
84					Rebecca	daughter			F	w	20	S	1901	al			yes	yes	Austria
85					Florence	daughter			F	w	18	S					yes	yes	New York
86					Mamie	daughter			F	w	15	S					yes	yes	New York
87					Morris	son			m	w	12	S				yes	yes	yes	New York
88				181	Hirshhorn Harry	Head 7	R		m	w	37	m	1912	Pa			yes	yes	Austria
89					Fanny	wife			F	w	31	m	1913	al			yes	yes	Austria
90				182	Kunzie Mary	Head 8	R		F	w	44	wd	1885	al			yes	yes	Austria
91					[illegible] Reinhart	son			m	w	[illegible]	S							[illegible]

***Census Record**: The 1920 New York City census contains valuable information about citizenship, including year of immigration; whether naturalized or alien; and, if naturalized, year of naturalization.*

BUREAU OF THE CENSUS

[D1–578]

ED STATES: 1920—POPULATION

SUPERVISOR'S DISTRICT NO. 1
ENUMERATION DISTRICT NO. 647
WARD OF CITY 8th

SHEET NO. 8 B

850

TED PLACE New York City (Insert proper name and, also, name of class, as city, village, town, or borough. See instructions.)

ERATED BY ME ON THE 15 DAY OF Jan 1920. Max Kern ENUMERATOR.

NATIVITY AND MOTHER TONGUE.						OCCUPATION.				
and parents of each person enumerated. If born in the United States, give the state or territory. If of foreign birth, give the place of birth and, in addition, the mother tongue. (See instructions.)	Father.		Mother.		Whether able to speak English.	Trade, profession, or particular kind of work done, as spinner, salesman, laborer, etc.	Industry, business, or establishment in which at work, as cotton mill, dry goods store, farm, etc.	Employer, salary or wage worker, or working on own account.	Number of farm schedule.	
Mother tongue.	Place of birth.	Mother tongue.	Place of birth.	Mother tongue.						
20	21	22	23	24	25	26	27	28	29	
English	Russia	Russian	Russia	Russian	yes					51
English	Russia	Russian	Russia	Russian	yes					52
Romania	Romania	Romanian	Romania	Romanian	yes	Peddler		OA		53
Romania	Romania	Romania	Romania	Romanian	yes	None				54
Romanian	Romania	Romanian	Romania	Romanian	yes	worker	factory	W		55
Romanian	Romania	Romanian	Romania	Romanian	yes	Conductor	Railroad	W		56
Romanian	Romania	Romanian	Romanian	Romanian	yes	Salesman	office	W		57
Romanian	Romania	Romanian	Romania	Romanian	yes	worker	office	W		58
Romanian	Romania	Romanian	Romania	Romanian	yes	Clerk	office	W		59
Austrian Ger	Austria	Austrian Ger	Austria	Austrian Ger	yes	Tailor	store	OA		60
Hungarian LC	Hungary	Hungarian LC	Hungary	Hungarian LC	yes	Painter	Bldg.	W		61
Russian	Russia	Russian	Russia	Russian	yes	Lawyer	office	OA		62
English	Hungary	Hungarian LC	Hungary	Hungarian LC	yes	None				63
English	Russia	Russian	New York	English						64
Austrian Ger	Austria	Austrian Ger	Austria	Austrian Ger	yes	Salesman	firm	W		65
Austrian Ger	Austria	Austrian Ger	Austria	Austrian Ger	yes	None				66
Austrian Ger	Austria	Austrian Ger	Austria	Austrian Ger	yes					67
Austrian Ger	Austria	Austrian Ger	Austria	Austrian LC	yes					68
Austrian Ger	Austria	Austrian Ger	Austria	Austrian Ger	yes					69
English	Russia	Russian	Russia	Russian	yes	officer	bank	W		70
Hungarian LC	Hungary	Hungarian LC	Hungary	Hungarian LC	yes	None				71
English	New York	English	Hungary	Hungarian	yes	None				72
English	New York	English	Hungary	Hungarian LC	yes					73
English	New York	English	Hungary	Hungarian LC	yes					74
English	New York	English	Hungary	Hungarian LC						75
Romanian	Romania	Romanian	Romania	Romanian	no	None				76
Romanian	Romania	Romanian	Romania	Romanian	yes	operator	shop	W		77
Romanian	Romania	Romanian	Romania	Romanian	yes	Painter	shop	W		78
Russian	Russia	Russian	Russia	Russian	yes	Painter	House	W		79
Russian	Russia	Russian	Russia	Russian	yes	None				80
English	Russia	Russian	Russia	Russian	yes					81
Russian	Russia	Russian	Russia	Russian	yes	dressmaker	shop	W		82
Austrian Ger	Austria	Austrian Ger	Austria	Austrian Ger	yes	None				83
Austrian Ger	Austria	Austrian Ger	Austria	Austrian Ger	yes	Stenographer	office	W		84
English	Austria	Austrian Ger	Austria	Austrian Ger	yes	Stenographer	office	W		85
English	Austria	Austrian Ger	Austria	Austrian Ger	yes	Clerk	office	W		86
English	Austria	Austrian Ger	Austria	Austrian Ger	yes	None				87
Austrian Ger	Austrian	Austrian Ger	Austria	Austrian Ger	yes	Dressmaker	shop	OA		88
Austrian Ger	Austria	Austrian Ger	Austria	Austrian Ger	yes	None				89
Austrian Ger	Austria	Austrian Ger	Austria	Austrian Ger	yes	None				90

JewishGen Family Finder

Run on Wednesday 1 September 1999 at 14:20:09

JewishGen's latest and most ambitious project involves traveling to your ancestral shtetl and documenting and preserving what you find there. Click here for more information on the 1999 programs.

Searching for Surname FINKELSTEIN

Number of hits: 140

This search request has been made possible through the *JewishGen-erosity* of
The JGS of Greater Washington in memory of Sheiala Moskow

Surname	Town	Country	Last Updated	Researcher (JGFF Code)
Finkelstein	Tirgu Neamt	Romania	Before 1997	Arye Barkai (#1020)
Finkelstein	Vaslui	Romania	Before 1997	
Finkelstein	Ivano Frankovsk	Ukraine	Before 1997	Nina C.R. Henry Price (#1042)
Finkelstein	Lviv	Ukraine	Before 1997	
Finkelstein	Marijampole	Lithuania	Before 1997	Michael Reynolds (#1064)
Finkelstein	Slavantai	Lithuania	Before 1997	
Finkelstein	Iasi	Romania	Before 1997	Gary Papush (#1191)
Finkelstein	Pamoitz	Lithuania	Before 1997	Richard Orkin (#1300)
Finkelstein	Pittsburgh, PA	USA	Before 1997	Delaine Winkler Shane (#1371)

***JewishGen Family Finder**: Internet data base containing the names of ancestral towns and surnames being researched by more than 30,000 genealogists worldwide. Shown here is information about person researching the surname Finkelstein.*

Avotaynu Soundex Search Result

The Data Bases column shows the codes for the various databases in which the surname appears. Scroll the screen down below the list of surnames to see the "List of Databases and Number of Surname Entries in CJSI". For each database, there is its code, followed by a brief description. This description has a link to a more detailed description of the database. Follow the link to learn how to access the database. Some databases are on-line, others are in books or microfiche.

Soundex	Name	Data Bases
765843	BANGELSDORF	B
765843	BENGELSDORF	ABCDGMZ
765843	BENGELSDORFF	P
765843	BENGIELSDORF	E
765843	FANKELSHTEJN	D
765843	FEINKELSTEIN	K
765843	FIENKELSTEIN	A
765843	FINCHELSTEIN	IK
765843	FINCKELSTEIN	CP
765843	FINKEELSTEIN	A
765843	FINKELCHTAIN	K
765843	FINKELSHTEIN	BCGZ
765843	FINKELSHTEJN	D
765843	FINKELSHTERN	D
765843	FINKELSHTOK	D
765843	FINKELSTEI	A
765843	FINKELSTEIN	ABCFGIJKLMNOPQTVYab
765843	FINKELSTEINAITI	K
765843	FINKELSTEINAS	I
765843	FINKELSTEINS	I
765843	FINKELSTEJN	CK
765843	FINKELSTINE	A
765843	FINKELSTON	A
765843	FINKELSTSEIN	P
765843	FINKELSZTAIN	L
765843	FINKELSZTEIN	KL
765843	FINKELSZTEJN	IK
765843	FINKIELSTAJN	K
765843	FINKIELSTEIN	IK
765843	FINKIELSTEJN	JK

[Show previous 30 records] [Show original 30 records] [Show next 30 records]

Enter a Surname for a new Search: [ ] Search Clear

List of Databases and Number of Surname Entries in CJSI

Visit our Home Page for more information about Avotaynu

- A. AJGS Cemetery Project Burials (51,453 surnames). 400,000 Jewish burials in various locations throughout the world.
- B. JewishGen Family Finder (28,411 surnames). Surnames being researched by some 12,000 Jewish genealogists worldwide.

Consolidated Jewish Surname Index*: Internet database which provides sources of information for more than 230,000 Jewish surnames. Shown are sources for the surname Finkelstein (and spelling variants). The Data Bases column contains codes for each of the databases included in the project whose description are shown below the list of surnames.*

Social Security Death Index Search Results

August 1999 Update - 61,964,627 records - Updated Monthly

The most full-featured and up-to-date SSDI search engine on the internet

Field	Value	Records	Results
Last Name	FINKELSTEIN	2485	2485
First Name	ABRAHAM	34155	45

Results 1 thru 15 of 45

Next

Name	Birth	Death	Last Residence	Last Benefit	SSN	Issued	Tools
ABRAHAM FINKELSTEIN	20 Sep 1897	Dec 1978	02116 (Boston, Suffolk, MA)	02146 (Brookline, Norfolk, MA)	018-14-0173	Massachusetts	SS-5 Letter Add Post-em
ABRAHAM FINKELSTEIN	28 Dec 1884	Oct 1971	02131 (Roslindale, Suffolk, MA)	(none specified)	030-16-2221	Massachusetts	SS-5 Letter Add Post-em
ABRAHAM FINKELSTEIN	15 Feb 1907	Jul 1979	90035 (Los Angeles, Los Angeles, CA)	90035 (Los Angeles, Los Angeles, CA)	034-24-9732	Massachusetts	SS-5 Letter Add Post-em
ABRAHAM FINKELSTEIN	12 Jun 1910	May 1982	11572 (Oceanside, Nassau, NY)	11572 (Oceanside, Nassau, NY)	050-01-0537	New York	SS-5 Letter Add Post-em
ABRAHAM FINKELSTEIN	24 Apr 1885	Oct 1968	11214 (Brooklyn, Kings, NY)	(none specified)	050-05-3936	New York	SS-5 Letter Add Post-em
ABRAHAM FINKELSTEIN	21 Mar 1911	Feb 1978	10016 (New York, New York, NY)	(none specified)	050-18-1374	New York	SS-5 Letter Add Post-em

***Social Security Death Index**: Internet database containing the names of some 60 million people for whom there was a Social Security death benefit claim starting in 1962. This illustrates a number of men named Abraham Finkelstein who appear in the database.*

***Tombstone Inscriptions**: The Hebrew inscription on a Jewish tombstones allows you to go back one additional generation, because it gives the name of the father of the deceased. This picture identifies three generations of Tartaskys. It is Manny Tartasky at the grave of his father, Me'er Tartasky, son of Yechazkel Tartasky.*

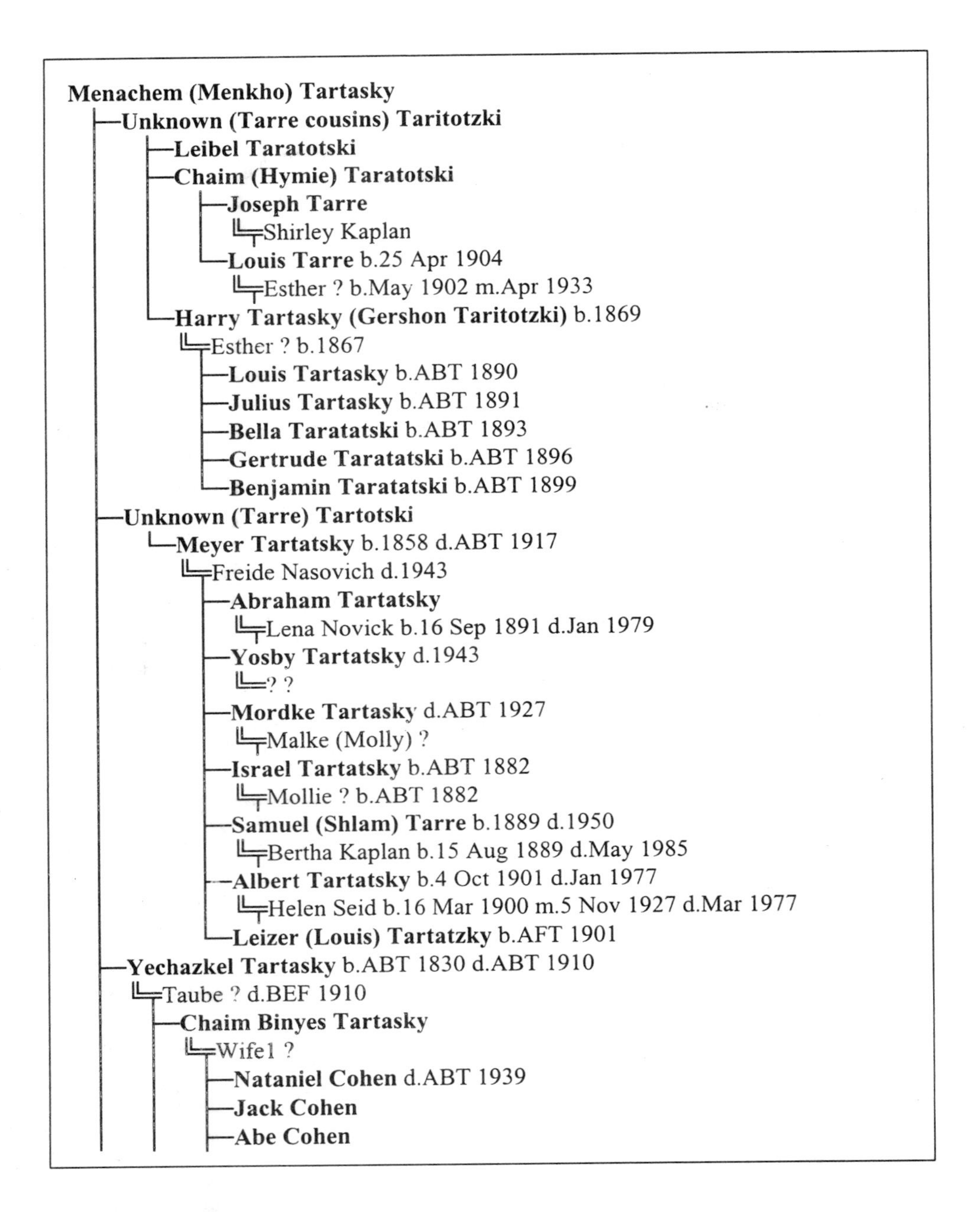

Descendancy Chart. *Genealogical software programs can produce a variety of reports and charts. This example, a descendancy chart, shows the progenitor on the top line and all descendants below, indenting one unit for every generation.*